THE NEW DECADE SERIES

PLAYBACK+
Speed • Pitch • Balance • Loop

SONGS OF 2010s

 68 Songs with Online Audio Backing Tracks

To access audio visit:
www.halleonard.com/mylibrary

Enter Code
7623-1972-1609-4422

ISBN 978-1-4950-4764-0

HAL•LEONARD® CORPORATION
7777 W. BLUEMOUND RD. P.O. BOX 13819 MILWAUKEE, WI 53213

For all works contained herein:
Unauthorized copying, arranging, adapting, recording, Internet posting, public performance,
or other distribution of the printed or recorded music in this publication is an infringement of copyright.
Infringers are liable under the law.

Visit Hal Leonard Online at
www.halleonard.com

4	The A Team	128	Firework
9	All About That Bass	134	Forget You
16	All of Me	142	Get Lucky
22	Animals	148	Happy
28	Baby	154	Hello
36	Bad Romance	160	Hey, Soul Sister
52	Best Day of My Life	121	Ho Hey
43	Blurred Lines	168	Home
60	Brave	175	The House That Built Me
66	Breakeven	182	I Knew You Were Trouble
82	Brighter Than the Sun	188	I Will Wait
90	Call Me Maybe	204	I Won't Give Up
94	Counting Stars	212	Jar of Hearts
75	Cruise	197	Just a Kiss
104	Cups (When I'm Gone)	220	Just Give Me a Reason
109	Earned It (Fifty Shades of Grey)	229	Just the Way You Are
114	Empire State of Mind	236	Lay Me Down

242	Let It Go	362	A Sky Full of Stars
262	Little Talks	376	Skyfall
251	Mean	382	Some Nights
272	Moves Like Jagger	392	Someone Like You
278	Need You Now	400	Stay
284	Paradise	406	Stay with Me
298	Pompeii	369	Stronger (What Doesn't Kill You)
304	Problem	410	Superheroes
293	Radioactive	417	Take Me to Church
310	Roar	424	Thinking Out Loud
315	Rolling in the Deep	436	A Thousand Years
324	Royals	429	Tonight Tonight
329	Say Something	444	Too Close
336	Secrets	470	Uptown Funk
342	See You Again	450	Wake Me Up!
349	Shake It Off	458	We Are Young
356	Shut Up and Dance	464	What Makes You Beautiful

ALL ABOUT THAT BASS

Words and Music by KEVIN KADISH
and MEGHAN TRAINOR

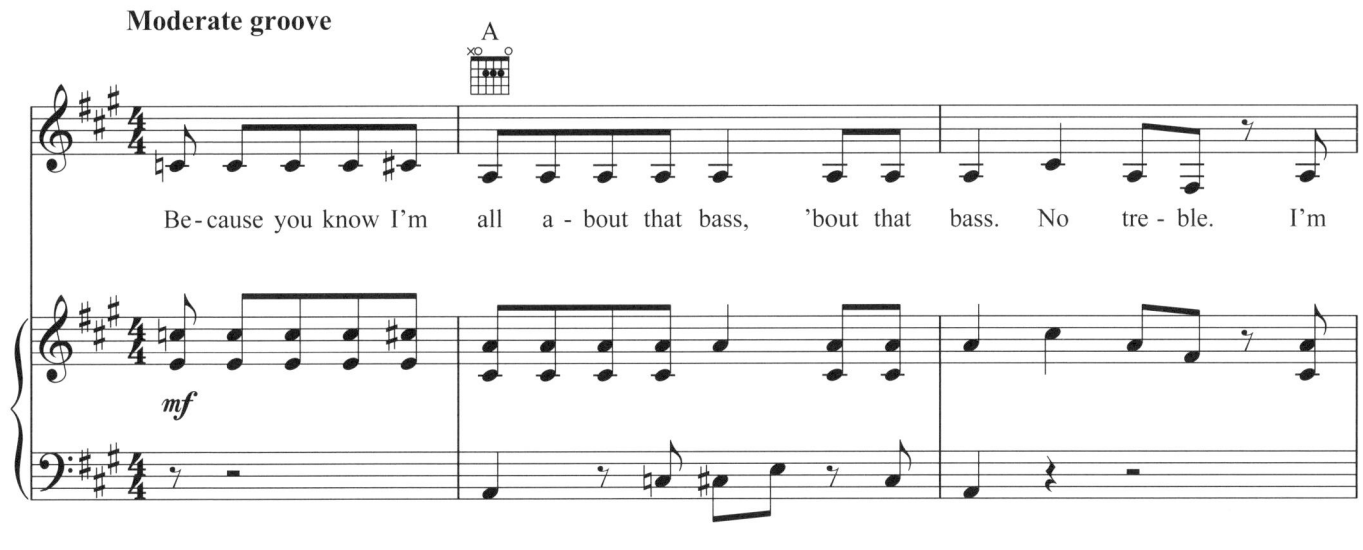

Copyright © 2014 Sony/ATV Music Publishing LLC, Over-Thought Under-Appreciated Songs, Year Of The Dog Music, a division of Big Yellow Dog, LLC and MTrain Music
All Rights on behalf of Sony/ATV Music Publishing LLC and Over-Thought Under-Appreciated Songs Administered by
Sony/ATV Music Publishing LLC, 424 Church Street, Suite 1200, Nashville, TN 37219
All Rights on behalf of Year Of The Dog Music, a division of Big Yellow Dog, LLC and MTrain Music Administered by Words & Music
International Copyright Secured   All Rights Reserved

ALL OF ME

Words and Music by JOHN STEPHENS
and TOBY GAD

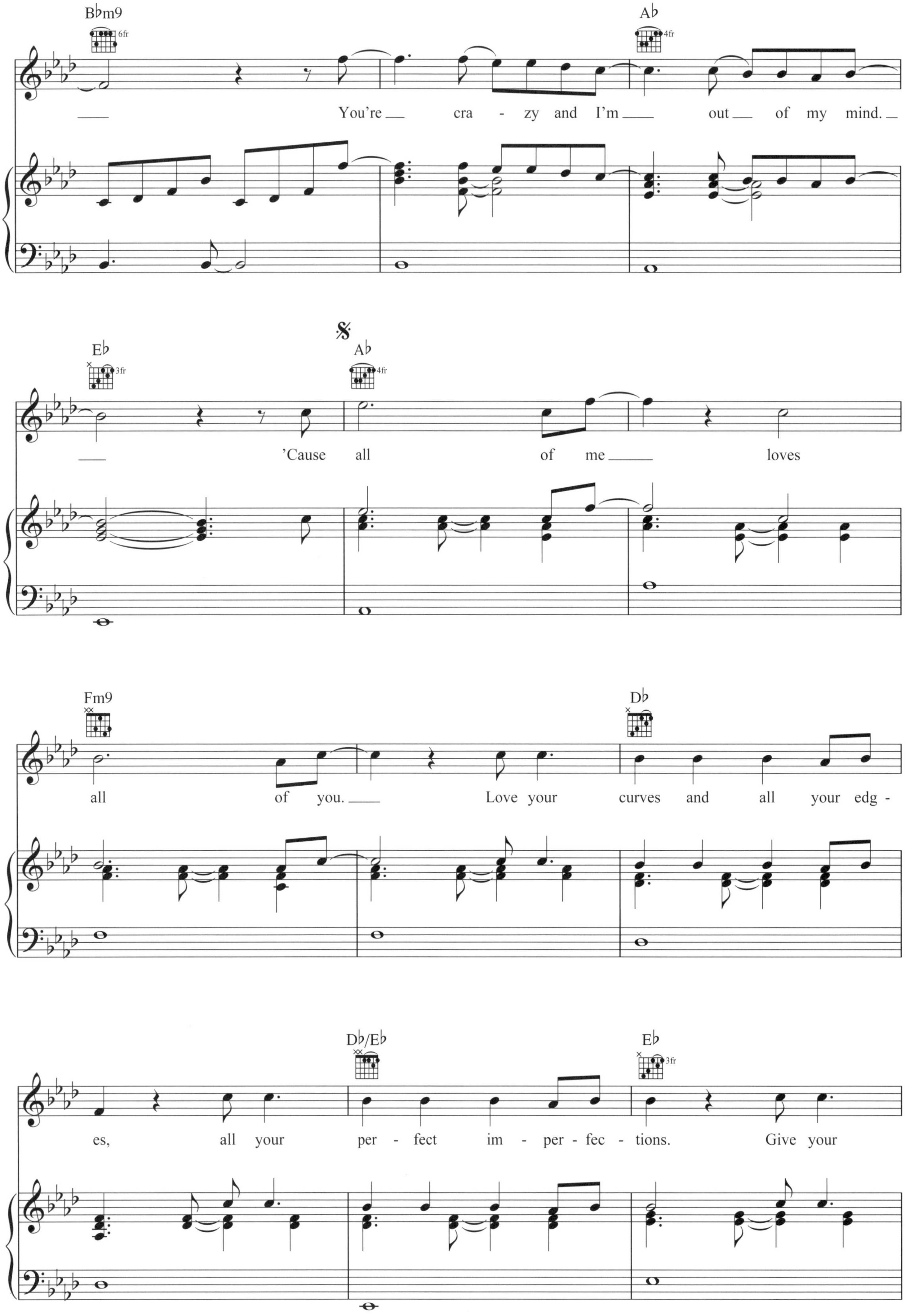
B♭m9
6fr
A♭
4fr
You're cra - zy and I'm out of my mind.
E♭
3fr
A♭
4fr
'Cause all of me loves
Fm9
D♭
all of you. Love your curves and all your edg -
D♭/E♭
E♭
3fr
es, all your per - fect im - per - fec - tions. Give your

ANIMALS

Words and Music by ADAM LEVINE,
BEN LEVIN and SHELLBACK

Ba-by, I'm prey-ing on you to-night,_ hunt you down, eat you a-live,_ just like

an - i - mals,_ an - i - mals,_ like an - i - mals,_ -mals._ May-be you

think that you can hide._ I can smell your scent for miles,_ just like

Copyright © 2014 Sudgee 2 Music, Matza Ballzack Music, Where Da Kasz At? and MXM Music AB
All Rights for Matza Ballzack Music Administered by Songs Of Universal, Inc.
All Rights for Where Da Kasz At? Administered Worldwide by Songs Of Kobalt Music Publishing
All Rights for MXM Music AB Administered Worldwide by Kobalt Songs Music Publishing
All Rights Reserved   Used by Permission

but I get so high when I'm in-side you.
that comes a-live when I'm in-side you. } Yeah, you can start

o-ver, you can run free, you can find oth-er fish in the sea. You can pre-

tend it's meant to be; but you can't stay a-way from me. I can still

hear you mak-ing that sound, tak-ing me down, roll-ing on the ground. You can pre-

BABY

Words and Music by JUSTIN BIEBER,
CHRISTOPHER STEWART, CHRISTINE FLORES,
CHRISTOPHER BRIDGES and TERIUS NASH

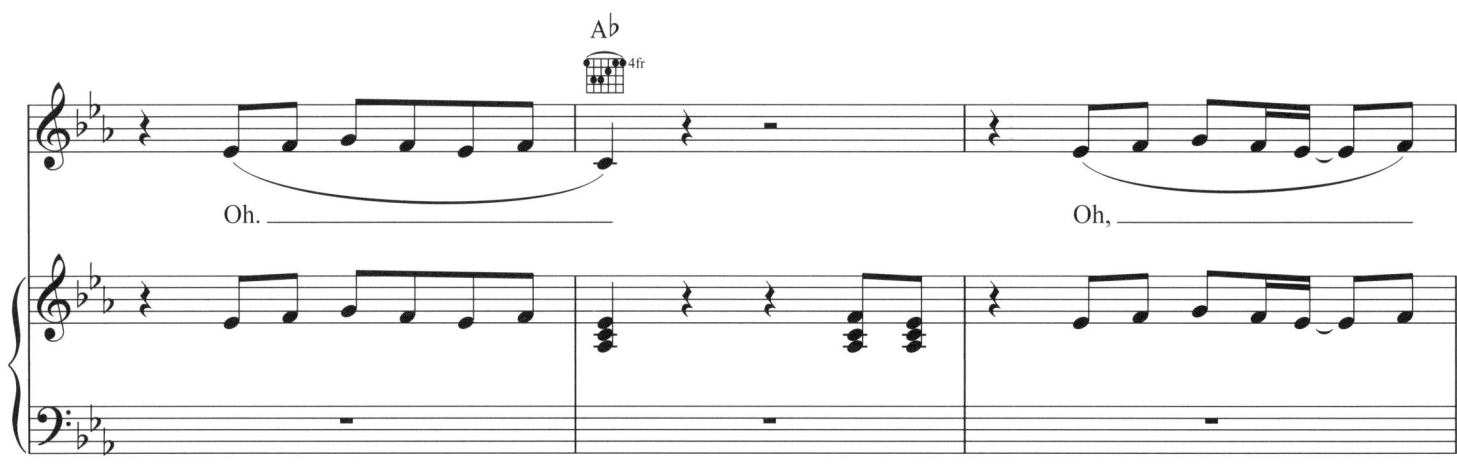

Copyright © 2010 UNIVERSAL MUSIC CORP., BIEBER TIME PUBLISHING, RZE MUSIC PUBLISHING, SONGS OF UNIVERSAL, INC.,
HAVANA BROWN PUBLISHING, LUDACRIS WORLDWIDE PUBLISHING, INC., WB MUSIC CORP. and 2082 MUSIC PUBLISHING
All Rights for BIEBER TIME PUBLISHING and RZE MUSIC PUBLISHING Controlled and Administered by UNIVERSAL MUSIC CORP.
All Rights for HAVANA BROWN PUBLISHING Controlled and Administered by SONGS OF UNIVERSAL, INC.
All Rights for LUDACRIS WORLDWIDE PUBLISHING, INC. Controlled and Administered by EMI APRIL MUSIC INC.
All Rights for 2082 MUSIC PUBLISHING Controlled and Administered by WB MUSIC CORP.
All Rights Reserved   Used by Permission

BAD ROMANCE

Words and Music by STEFANI GERMANOTTA
and NADIR KHAYAT

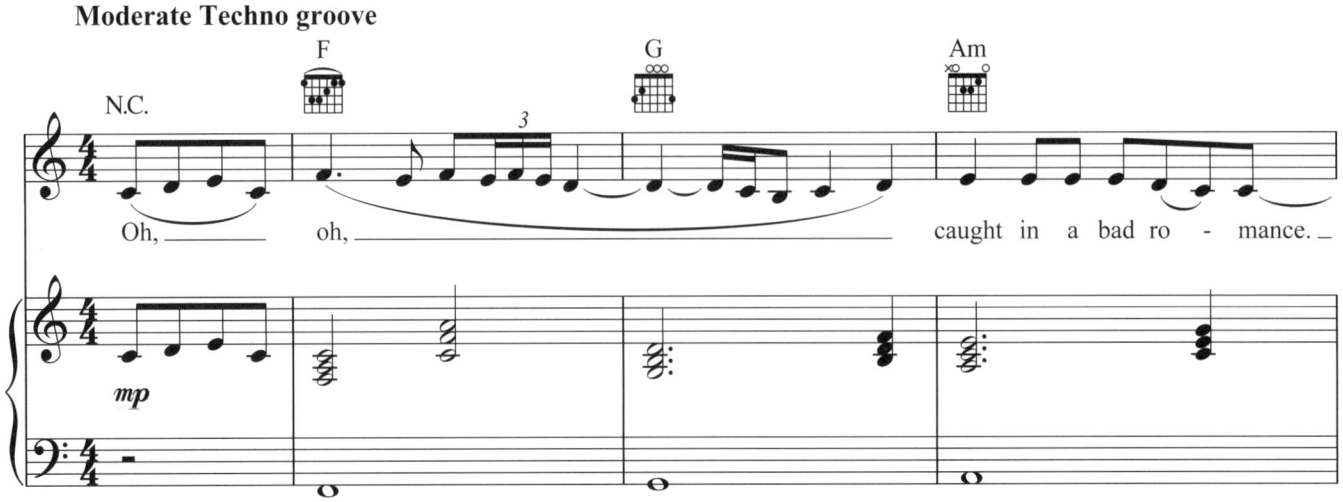

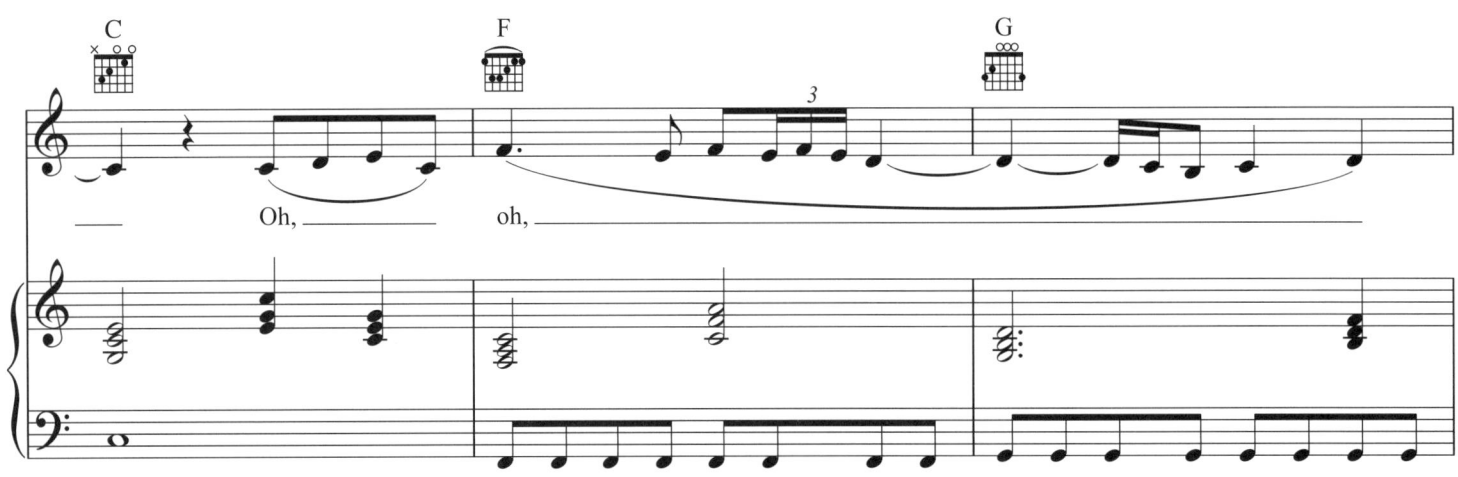

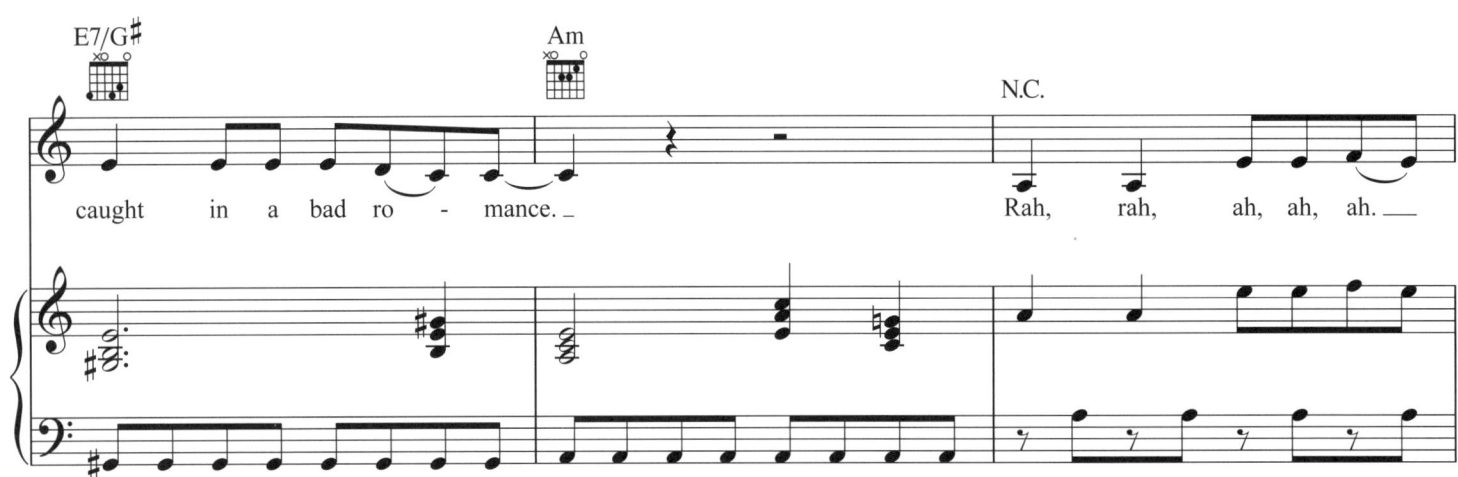

Copyright © 2009 Sony/ATV Music Publishing LLC and House Of Gaga Publishing Inc.
All Rights Administered by Sony/ATV Music Publishing LLC, 424 Church Street, Suite 1200, Nashville, TN 37219
International Copyright Secured   All Rights Reserved

BLURRED LINES

Words and Music by PHARRELL WILLIAMS,
ROBIN THICKE and CLIFFORD HARRIS

Moderate groove

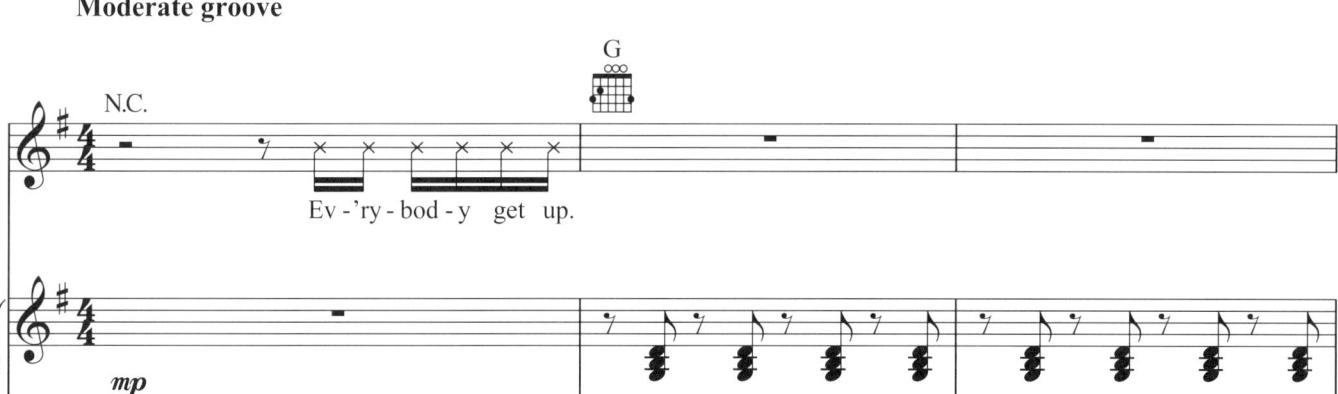

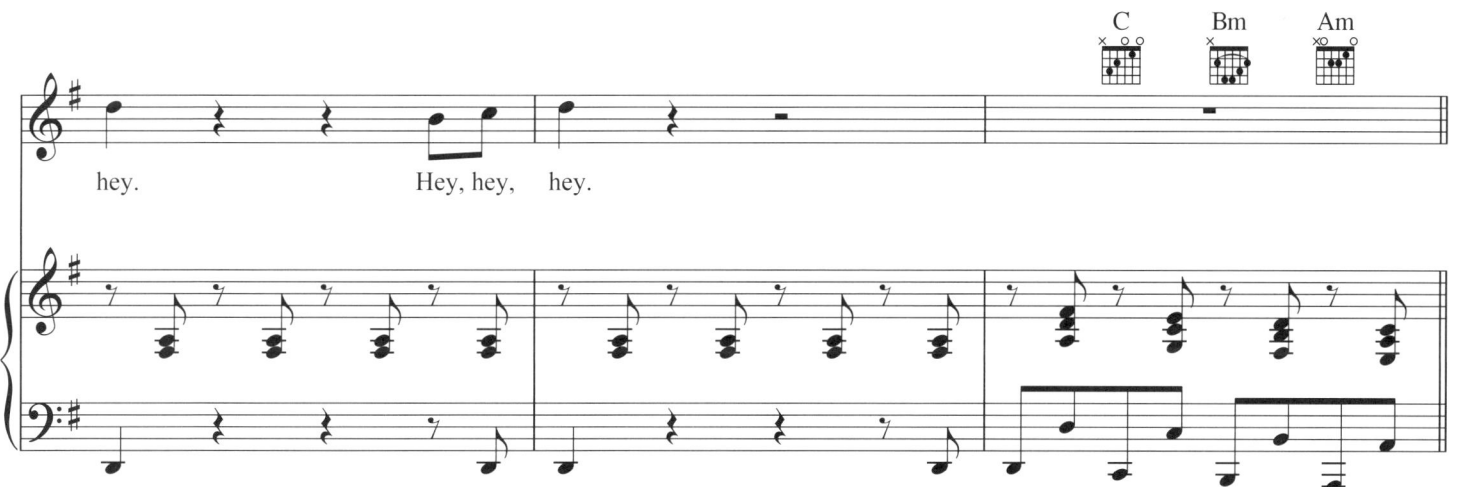

Copyright © 2013 EMI April Music Inc., More Water From Nazareth, Deyjah's Daddy Muzik and I Like 'Em Thicke Music
All Rights on behalf of EMI April Music Inc., More Water From Nazareth and Deyjah's Daddy Musik Administered by
Sony/ATV Music Publishing LLC, 424 Church Street, Suite 1200, Nashville, TN 37219
International Copyright Secured   All Rights Reserved

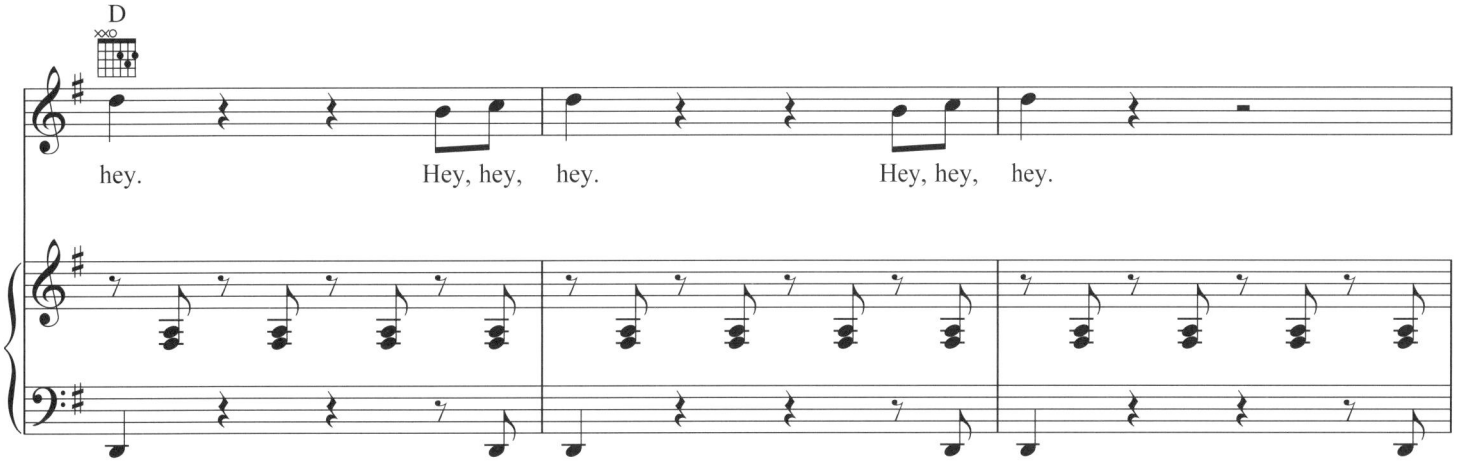
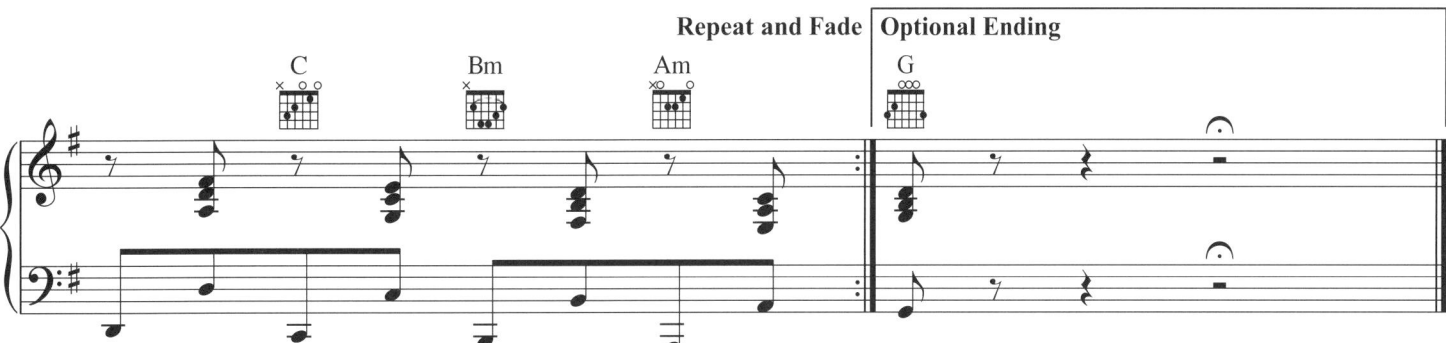

Additional Lyrics

Rap: One thing I ask of you, let me be the one you back that ass to.
Yo, from Malibu to Paribu, yeah, had a bitch, but she ain't bad as you.
So, hit me up when you pass through, I give you something big enough to tear your ass in two.
Swag on 'em even when you dress casual. I mean, it's almost unbearable.
In a hundred year, not dare would I pull a Pharcide bitch, you pass me by.
I'm nothing like your last guy, he too square for you. He don't smack that ass and pull your hair for you.
So I'm just watchin' and waitin' for you to salute the truly pimpin'.
Not many women can refuse this pimpin'. I'm a nice guy, but don't get it confused, you gettin' it.

BEST DAY OF MY LIFE

Words and Music by ZACHARY BARNETT,
JAMES ADAM SHELLEY, MATTHEW SANCHEZ,
DAVID RUBLIN, SHEP GOODMAN
and AARON ACCETTA

Pop Rock

Copyright © 2013 Round Hill Copyrights, Zachary Barnett Publishing, James Adam Shelley Publishing, Round Hill Works, Dave Rublin Publishing,
Owl And Fox Publishing, EMI April Music Inc., DRAWOC, Sony/ATV Allegro and Needledown Publishing
All Rights on behalf of itself, Zachary Barnett Publishing and James Adam Shelley Publishing Controlled and Administered by Round Hill Copyrights (SESAC)
All Rights on behalf of itself, Dave Rublin Publishing and Owl And Fox Publishing Controlled and Administered by Round Hill Works (BMI)
All Rights on behalf of EMI April Music Inc., DRAWOC, Sony/ATV Allegro and Needledown Publishing Administered by
Sony/ATV Music Publishing LLC, 424 Church Street, Suite 1200, Nashville, TN 37219
International Copyright Secured   All Rights Reserved

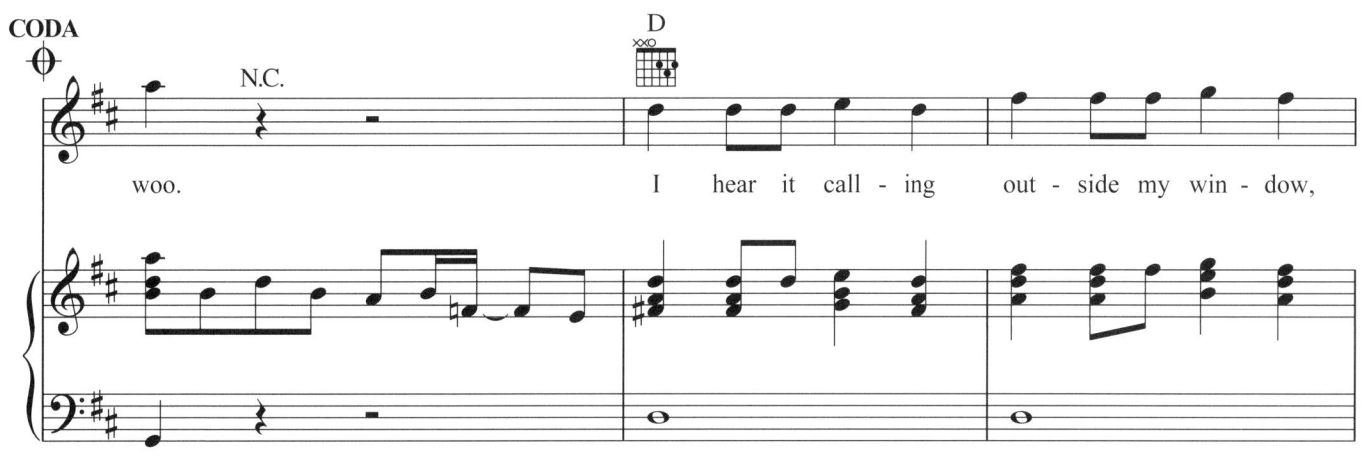

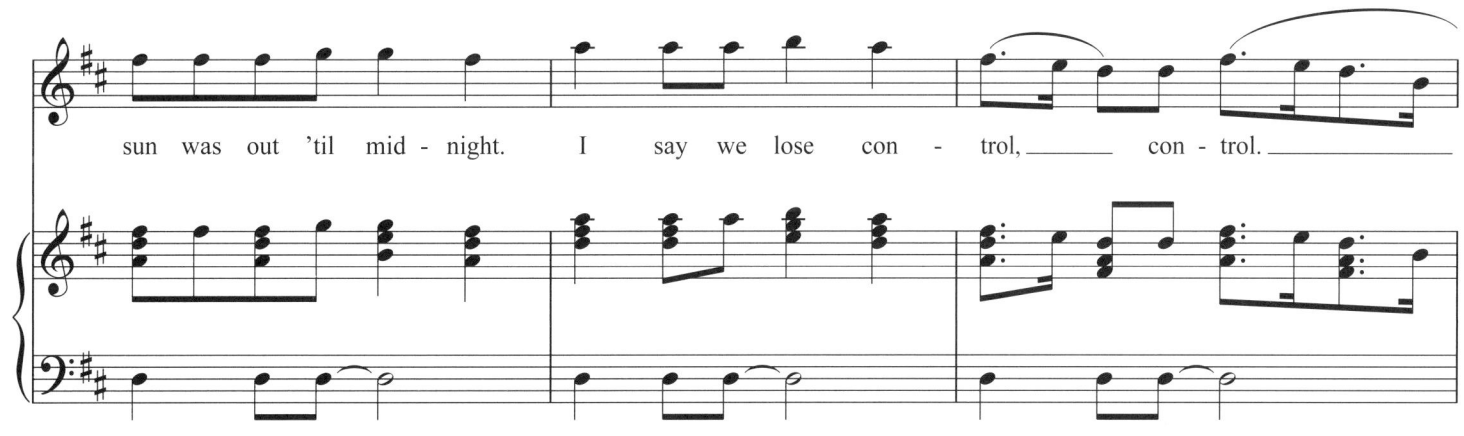

BRAVE

Words and Music by SARA BAREILLES
and JACK ANTONOFF

Moderately

You can be a-maz-in', you can turn a phrase in-to a wea-pon or a drug.

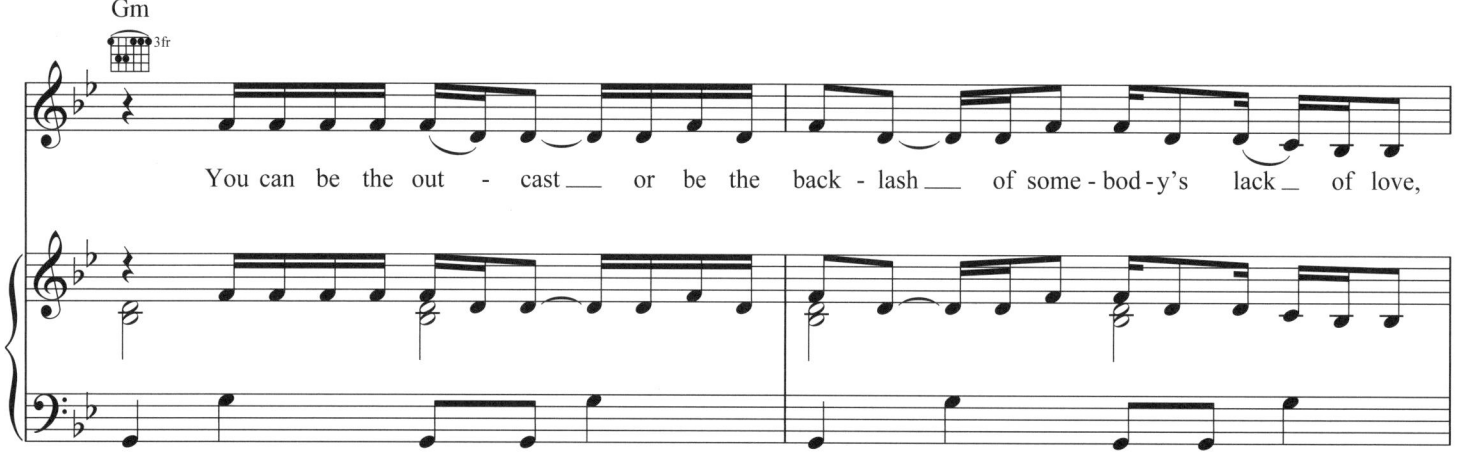

You can be the out-cast or be the back-lash of some-bod-y's lack of love,

or you can start speak-ing up.

Copyright © 2013 Sony/ATV Music Publishing LLC, Tiny Bear Music and Ducky Donath Music
All Rights Administered by Sony/ATV Music Publishing LLC, 424 Church Street, Suite 1200, Nashville, TN 37219
International Copyright Secured All Rights Reserved

BREAKEVEN

Words and Music by STEPHEN KIPNER, ANDREW FRAMPTON, DANIEL O'DONOGHUE and MARK SHEEHAN

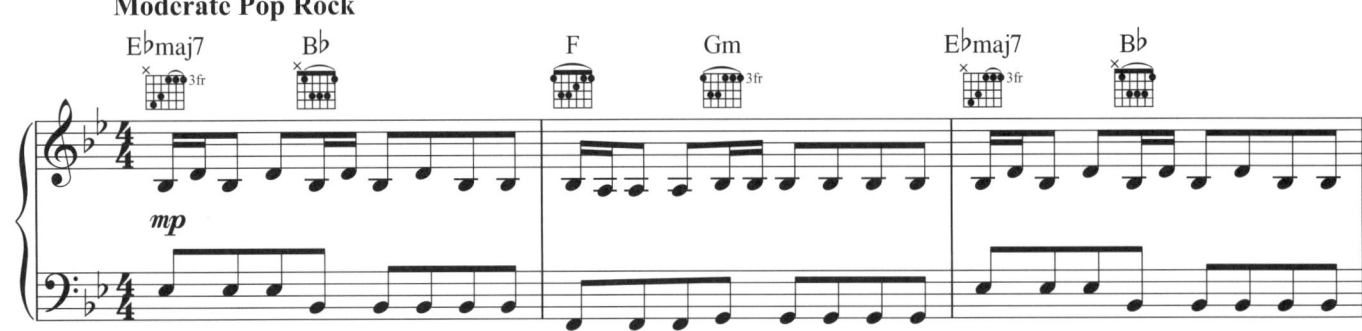

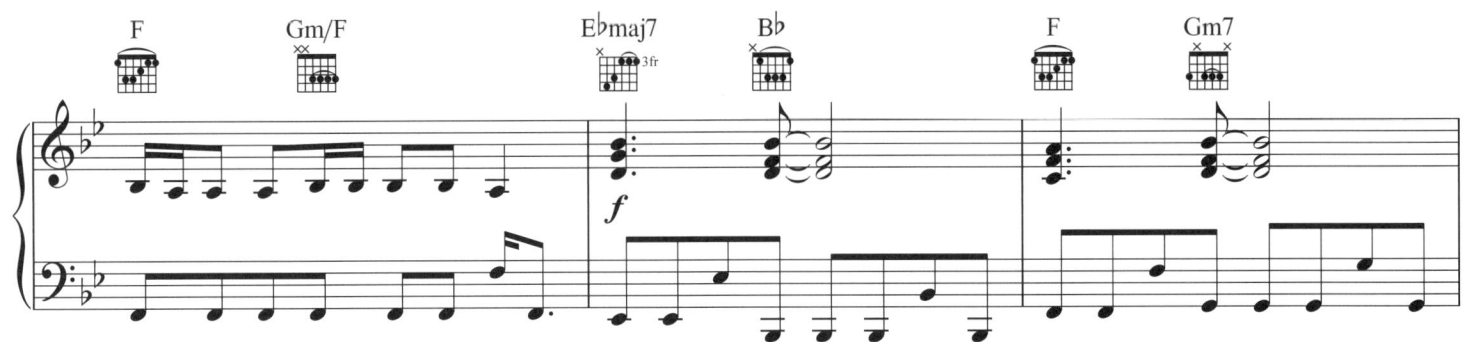

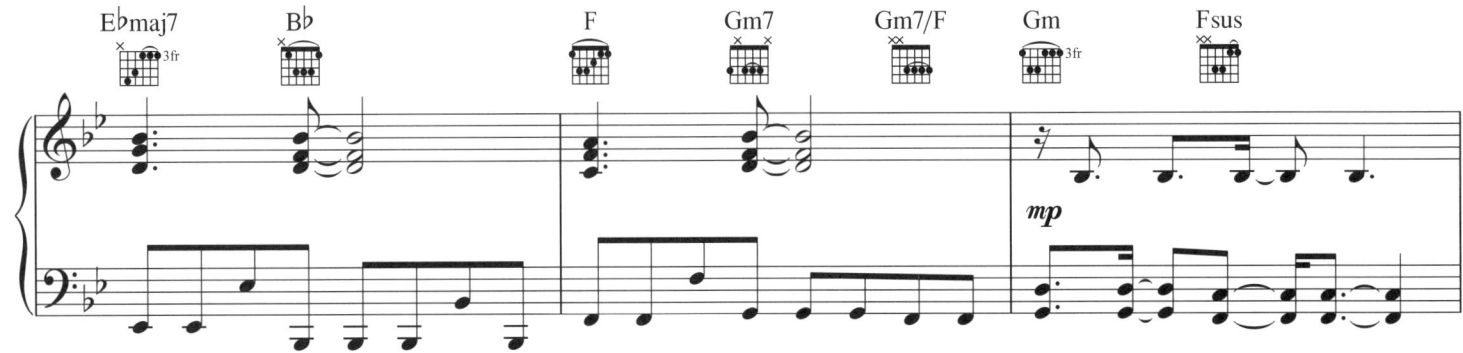

I'm still a-live but I'm bare-ly breath-in',

© 2008 EMI APRIL MUSIC INC., SONIC GRAFFITI, ANDREW FRAMPTON MUSIC and UNIVERSAL MUSIC - Z SONGS
All Rights for SONIC GRAFFITI Controlled and Administered by EMI APRIL MUSIC INC.
All Rights for ANDREW FRAMPTON MUSIC Administered by STAGE THREE MUSIC (US) INC., A BMG COMPANY
All Rights Reserved   International Copyright Secured   Used by Permission

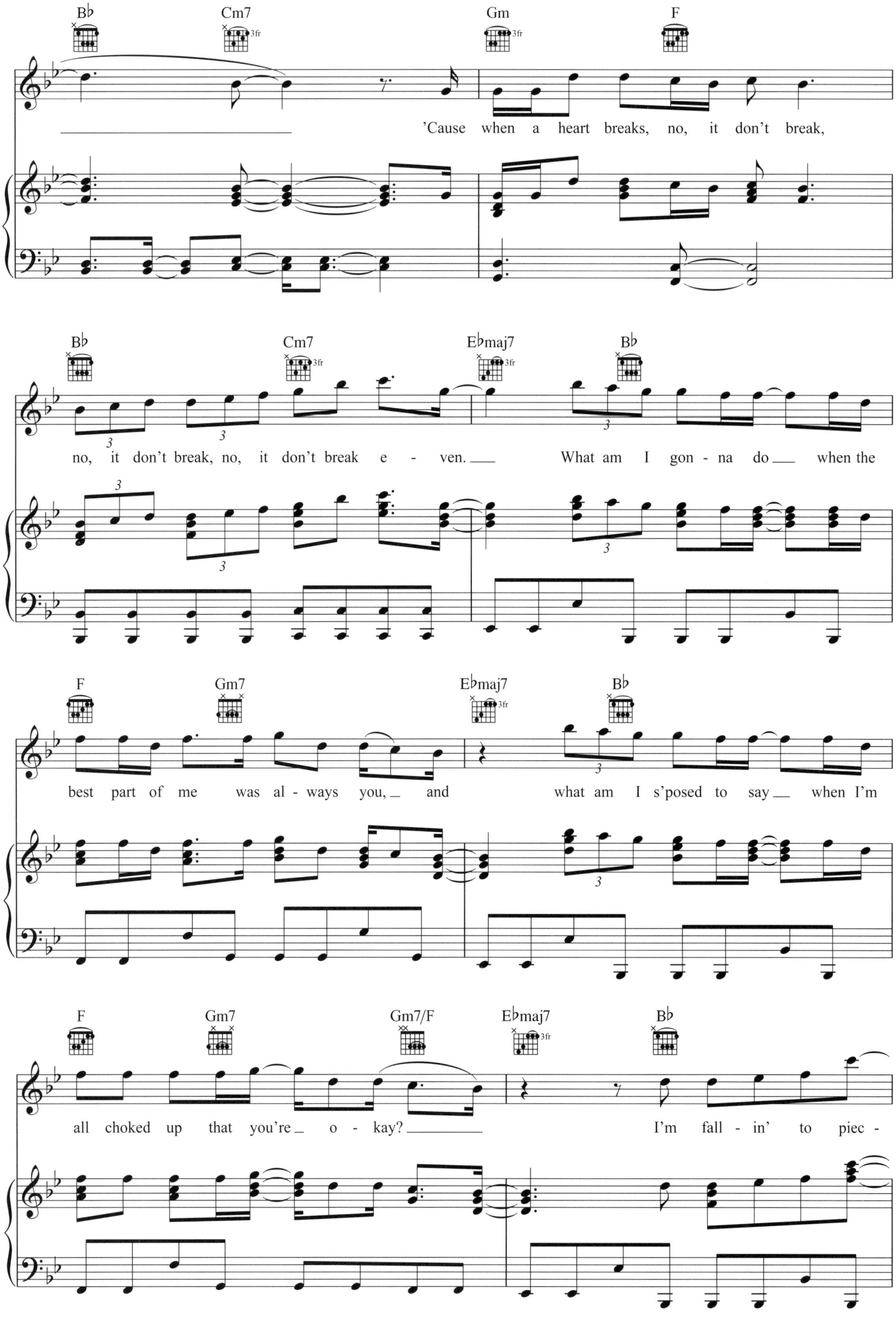
B♭ Cm7 Gm F
3fr
'Cause when a heart breaks, no, it don't break,
B♭ Cm7 E♭maj7 B♭
no, it don't break, no, it don't break e - ven. What am I gon - na do when the
F Gm7 E♭maj7 B♭
best part of me was al - ways you, and what am I s'posed to say when I'm
F Gm7 Gm7/F E♭maj7 B♭
all choked up that you're o - kay? I'm fall - in' to piec -

CRUISE

Words and Music by CHASE RICE,
TYLER HUBBARD, BRIAN KELLEY,
JOEY MOI and JESSE RICE

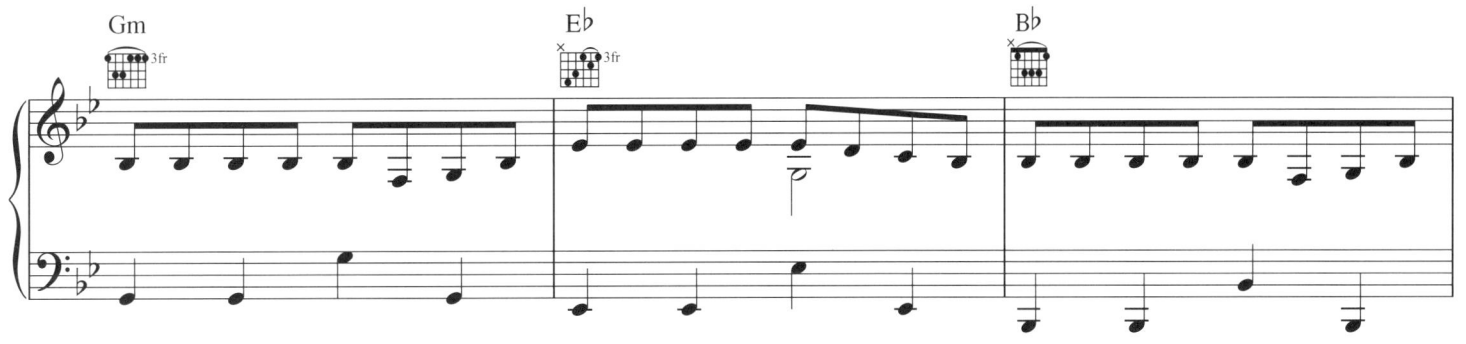

Copyright © 2012 Sony/ATV Music Publishing LLC, Dack Janiels Publishing, Big Loud Mountain, Big Red Toe, Deep Fried Dreams and Artist Revolution Publishing
All Rights on behalf of Sony/ATV Music Publishing LLC and Dack Janiels Publishing Administered by Sony/ATV Music Publishing LLC, 424 Church Street, Suite 1200, Nashville, TN 37219
All Rights on behalf of Big Loud Mountain, Big Red Toe and Deep Fried Dreams Administered by Big Loud Bucks
All Rights on behalf of Artist Revolution Publishing Administered by Ole
International Copyright Secured All Rights Reserved

BRIGHTER THAN THE SUN

Words and Music by COLBIE CAILLAT
and RYAN TEDDER

Copyright © 2011 Plummy Lou Music (BMI) and Write 2 Live (ASCAP)
All Rights for Write 2 Live Administered by Kobalt Songs Music Publishing
International Copyright Secured   All Rights Reserved

CALL ME MAYBE

Words and Music by CARLY RAE JEPSEN,
JOSHUA RAMSAY and TAVISH CROWE

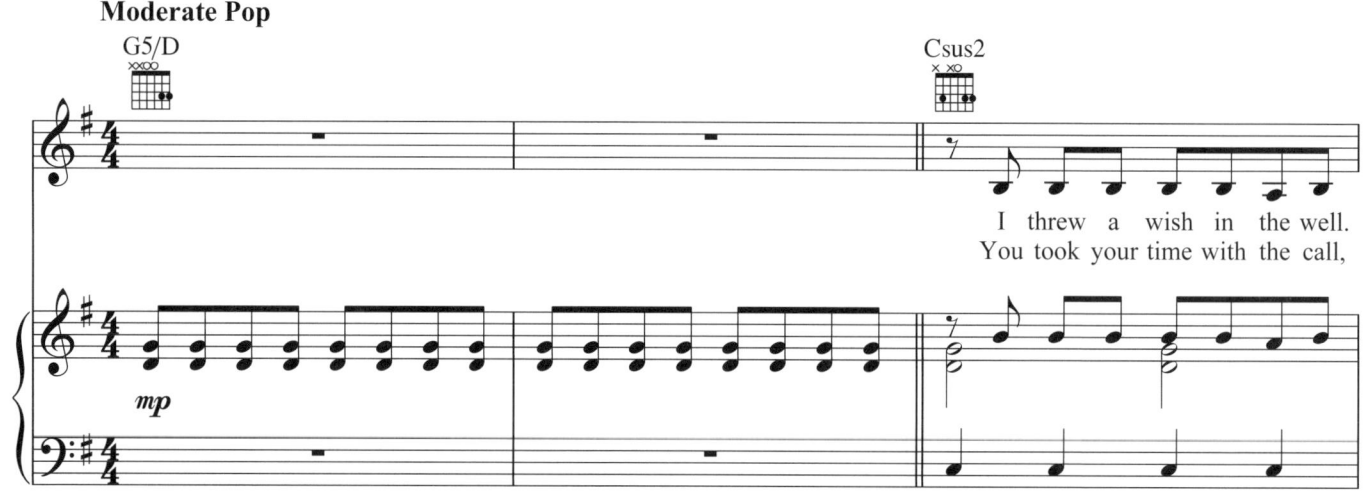

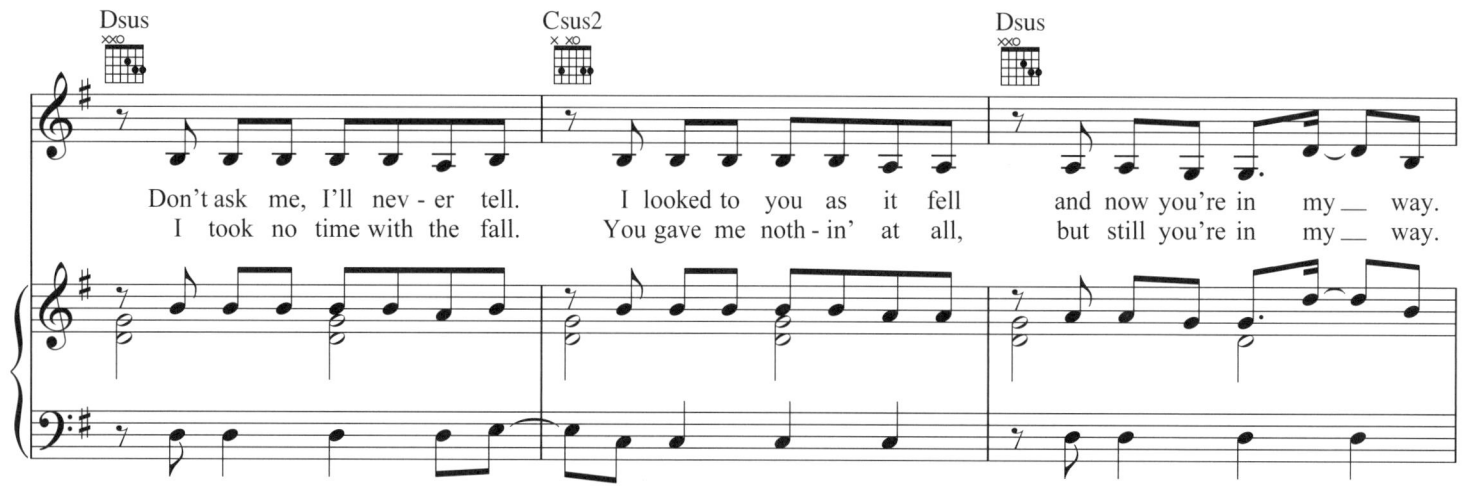

Copyright © 2011 UNIVERSAL MUSIC CORP., JEPSEN MUSIC PUBLISHING, BMG GOLD SONGS, CROWE MUSIC INC. and BMG PLATINUM SONGS
All Rights for JEPSEN MUSIC PUBLISHING Controlled and Administered by UNIVERSAL MUSIC CORP.
All Rights for BMG GOLD SONGS, CROWE MUSIC INC. and BMG PLATINUM SONGS Administered by BMG RIGHTS MANAGEMENT (US) LLC
All Rights Reserved   Used by Permission

COUNTING STARS

Words and Music by
RYAN TEDDER

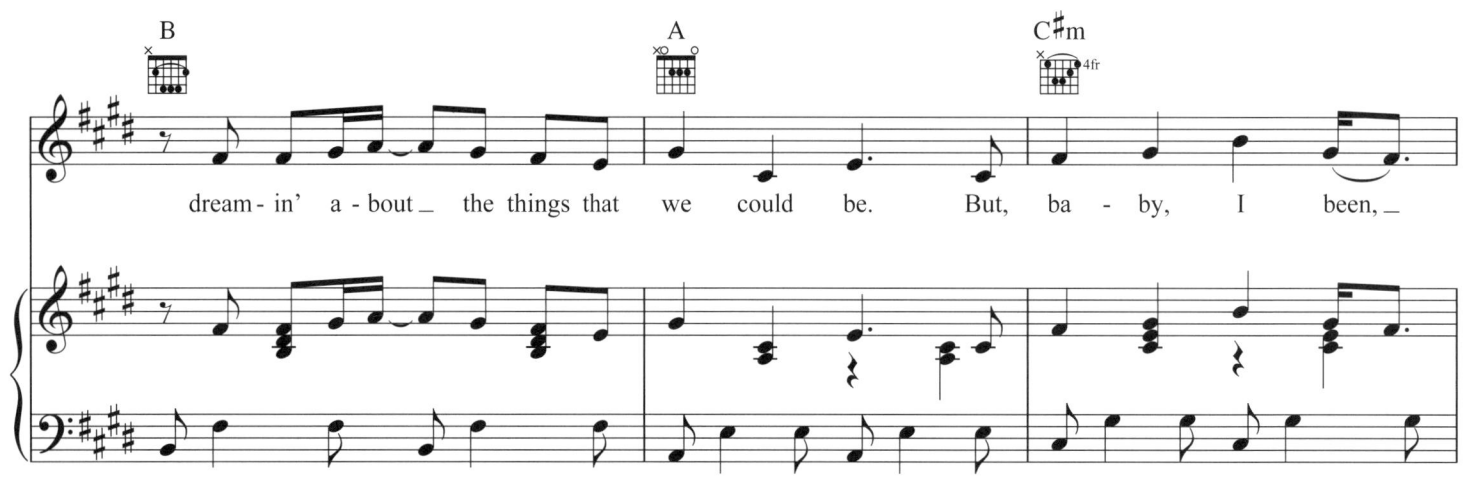

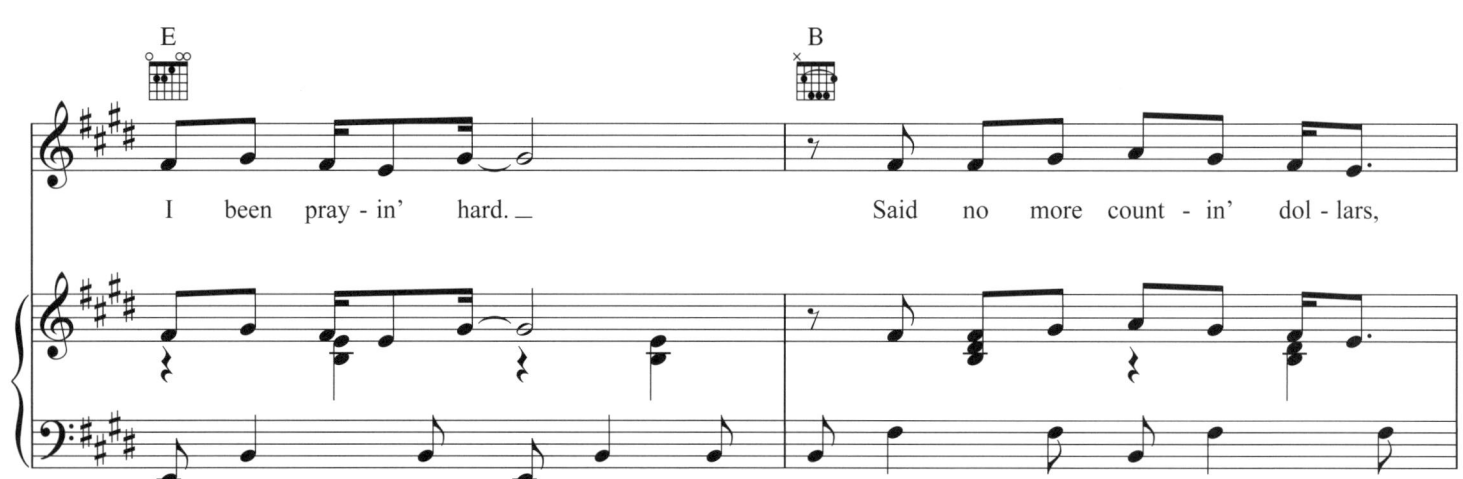

Copyright © 2013 Sony/ATV Music Publishing LLC, Velvet Hammer Music and Midnite Miracle Music
All Rights Administered by Sony/ATV Music Publishing LLC, 424 Church Street, Suite 1200, Nashville, TN 37219
International Copyright Secured   All Rights Reserved

CUPS
(When I'm Gone)
from the Motion Picture Soundtrack PITCH PERFECT

Words and Music by A.P. CARTER,
LUISA GERSTEIN and HELOISE TUNSTALL-BEHRENS

Moderate Folk

I got my tick-et for the long way 'round,

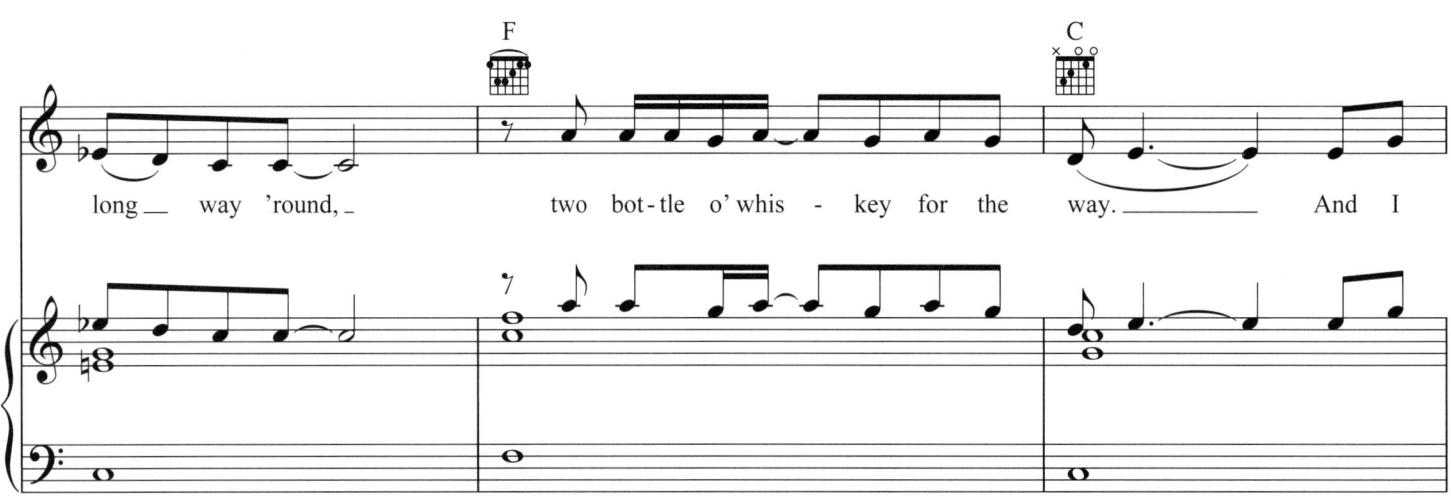

two bot-tle o' whis-key for the way. And I sure would like some sweet com-pa-ny. And I'm leav-in' to-mor-row, what do ya

Copyright © 2013 by Peer International Corporation and BMG Gold Songs
All Rights for BMG Gold Songs Administered by BMG Rights Management (US) LLC
International Copyright Secured   All Rights Reserved
- contains a sample from "When I'm Gone" by A.P. Carter

EARNED IT
(Fifty Shades of Grey)
from FIFTY SHADES OF GREY

Words and Music by ABEL TESFAYE, AHMAD BALSHE, STEPHAN MOCCIO and JASON QUENNEVILLE

Copyright © 2015 Songs Music Publishing, LLC o/b/o Songs Of SMP, Universal Pictures Music, U.P.G. Music Publishing,
Sing Little Penguin, Universal Music Corp., CP Music Group, Inc. and WB Music Corp.
All Rights for Universal Pictures Music Administered by Universal Music Corp.
All Rights for U.P.G. Music Publishing and Sing Little Penguin Administered by Songs Of Universal, Inc.
All Rights for CP Music Group, Inc. Administered by Universal Music Corp. and WB Music Corp.
All Rights Reserved Used by Permission

EMPIRE STATE OF MIND

Words and Music by ALICIA KEYS, SHAWN CARTER,
JANE'T SEWELL, ANGELA HUNTE, AL SHUCKBURGH,
BERT KEYES and SYLVIA ROBINSON

Moderate Hip-Hop

1. Yeah, yeah, I'm up at

Brook-lyn, now I'm down in Tri-bec-a, right next to De Ni-ro, but I'll be hood for-ev-er. I'm the new Si-
2., 3. (See Rap lyrics)

© 2009 EMI APRIL MUSIC INC., LELLOW PRODUCTIONS, CARTER BOYS MUSIC, J SEWELL PUBLISHING, EMI FORAY MUSIC,
MASANI ELSHABAZZ MUSIC, GLOBAL TALENT PUBLISHING, TWENTY NINE BLACK MUSIC, GAMBI MUSIC INC., ROC COR PUBLISHING and SUGAR HILL MUSIC PUBLISHING
All Rights for LELLOW PRODUCTIONS, CARTER BOYS MUSIC and J SEWELL PUBLISHING Controlled and Administered by EMI APRIL MUSIC INC.
All Rights for MASANI ELSHABAZZ MUSIC Controlled and Administered by EMI FORAY MUSIC
All Rights for GLOBAL TALENT PUBLISHING Administered by DOWNTOWN MUSIC PUBLISHING LLC
All Rights Reserved   International Copyright Secured   Used by Permission
- contains elements of "Love On A Two Way Street" (Keyes/Robinson) © 1970 Twenty Nine Black Music and Gambi Music Inc

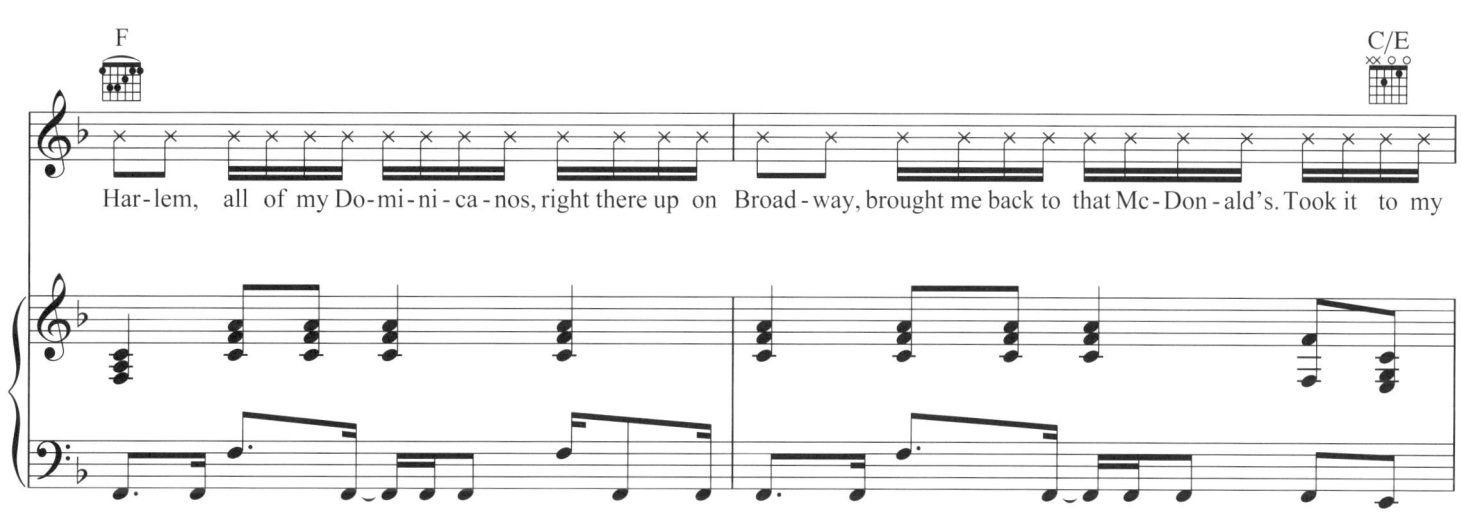
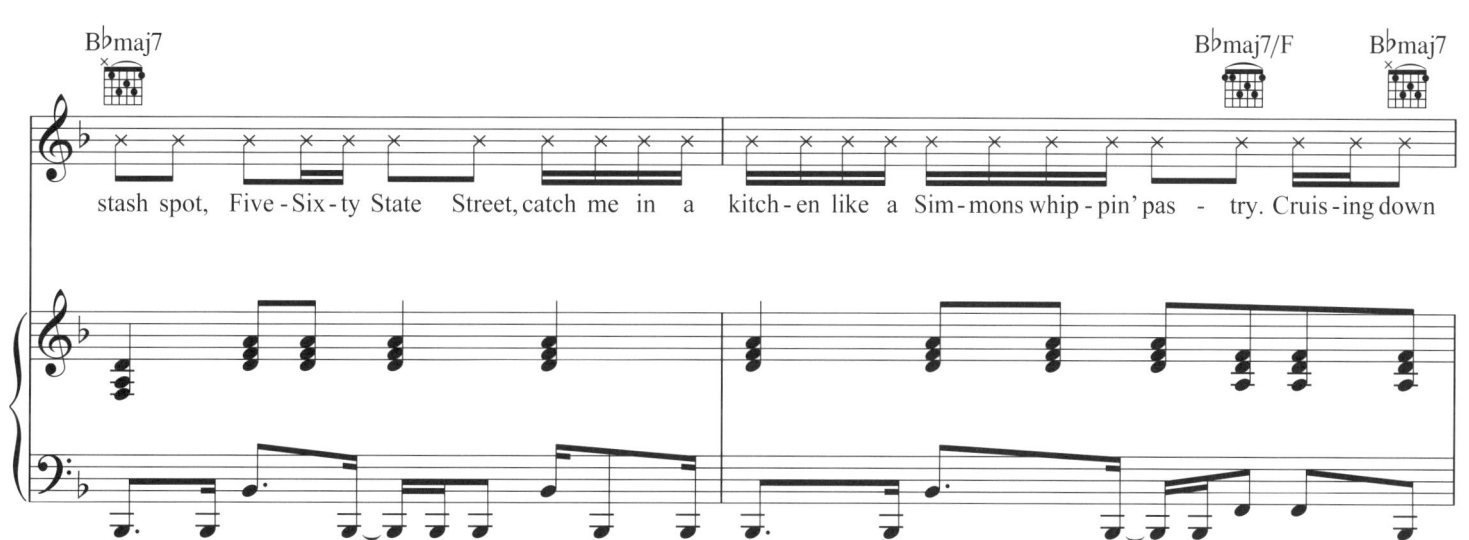

117

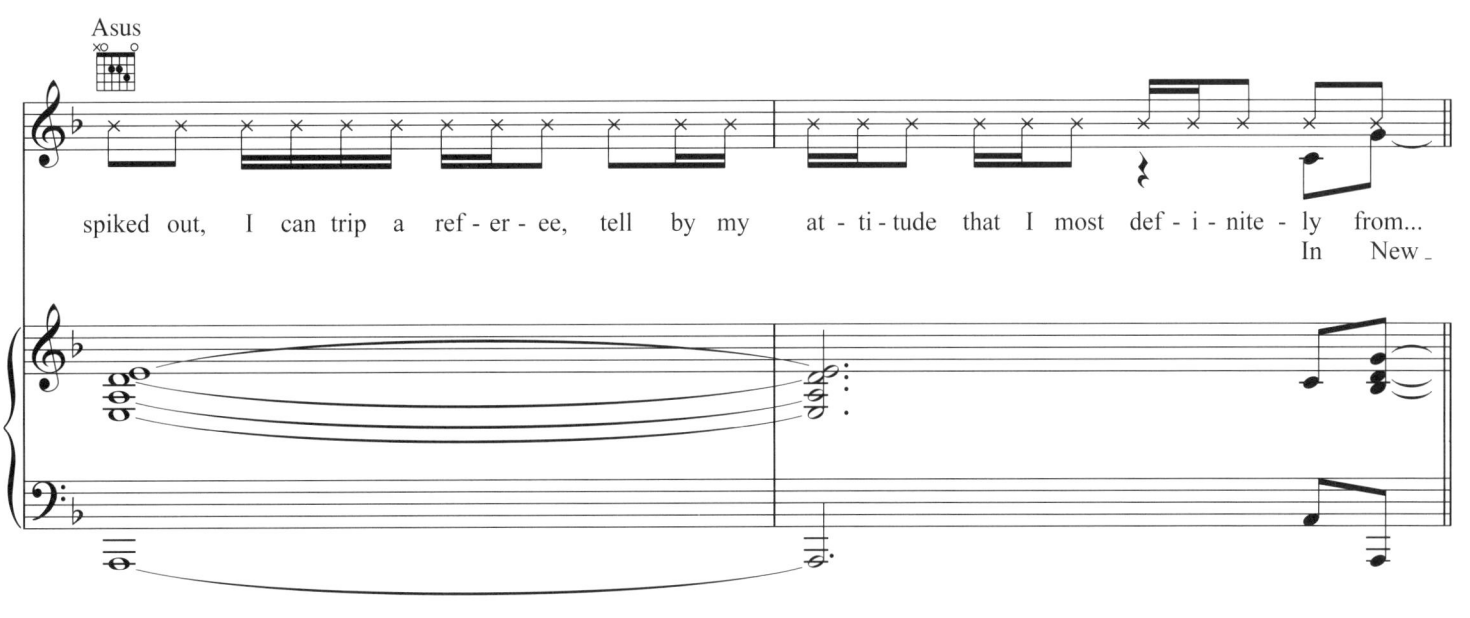

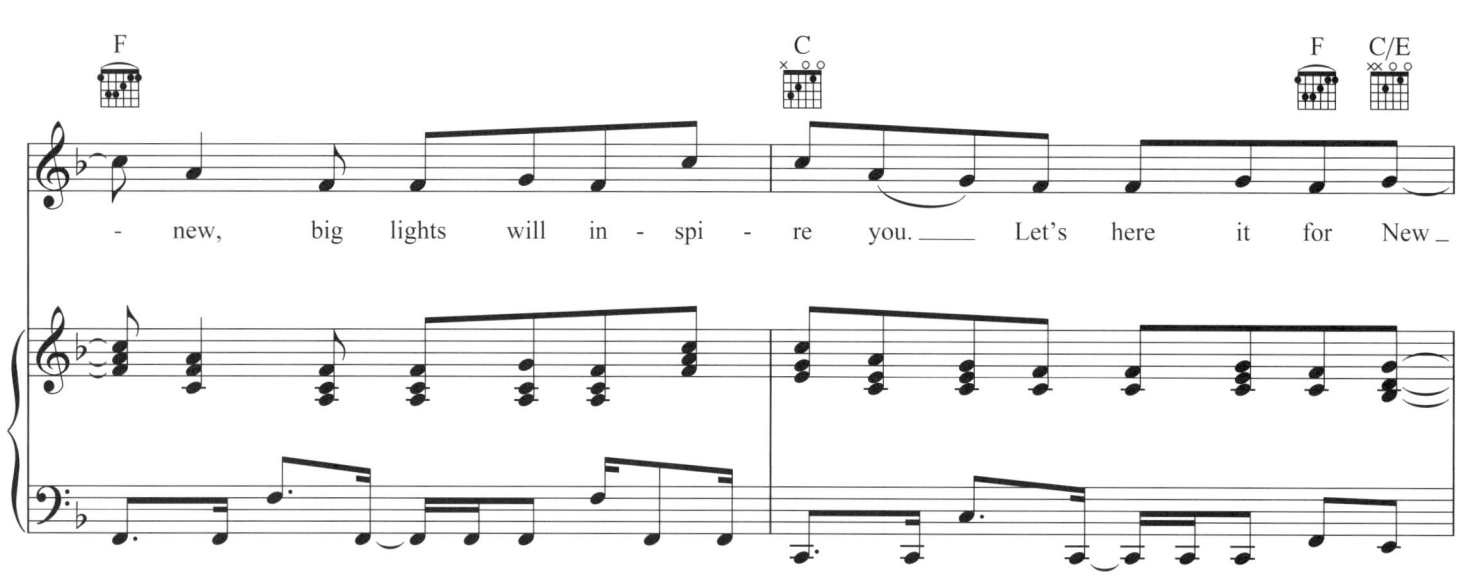

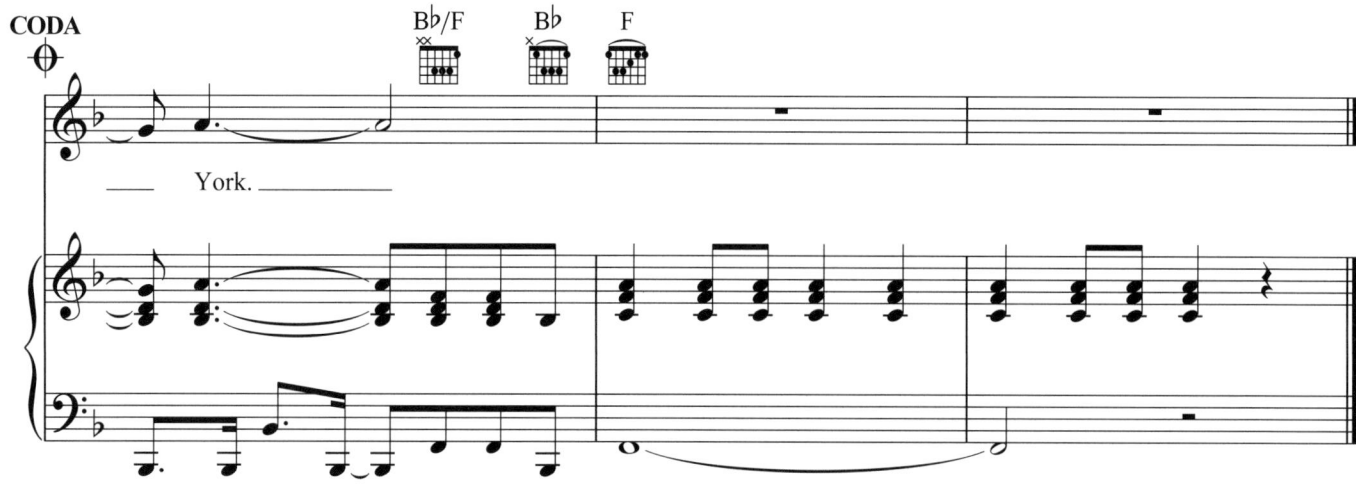

Rap Lyrics

2. Catch me at the X with OG at a Yankee game.
   Dude, I made the Yankee hat more famous than a Yankee can.
   You should know I bleed blue, but I ain't a crip though,
   But I got a gang of brothas walking with my clique though.

   Welcome to the melting pot, corners where we selling rocks,
   Afrika bambaataa, home of the hip-hop,
   Yellow cab, gypsy cab, dollar cab, holla back,
   For foreigners it ain't for they act like they forgot how to act.

   Eight million stories out there and they're naked.
   City, it's a pity half of y'all won't make it.
   Me, I gotta plug Special Ed, I got it made,
   If Jeezy's paying LeBron, I'm paying Dwyane Wade.

   3 dice, Cee Lo, 3-Card Monte,
   Labor Day parade, rest in peace Bob Marley.
   Statue of Liberty, long live the World Trade,
   Long live the King, yo, I'm from the Empire State that's...

3. Lights is blinding, girls need blinders
   So they can step out of bounds quick.
   The sidelines is blind with casualties, who sip your life casually,
   Then gradually become worse. Don't bite the apple, Eve.

   Caught up in the in-crowd, now you're in style,
   And in the winter gets cold, en vogue with your skin out.
   The city of sin is a pity on a whim,
   Good girls gone bad, the city's filled with them.

   Mami took a bus trip, now she got her bust out,
   Everybody ride her, just like a bus route.
   Hail Mary to the city, you're a virgin,
   And Jesus can't save you, life starts when the church in.

   Came here for school, graduated to the high life.
   Ball players, rap stars, addicted to the limelight.
   MD, MA got you feeling like a champion,
   The city never sleeps, better slip you a Ambien.

HO HEY

Words and Music by JEREMY FRAITES
and WESLEY SCHULTZ

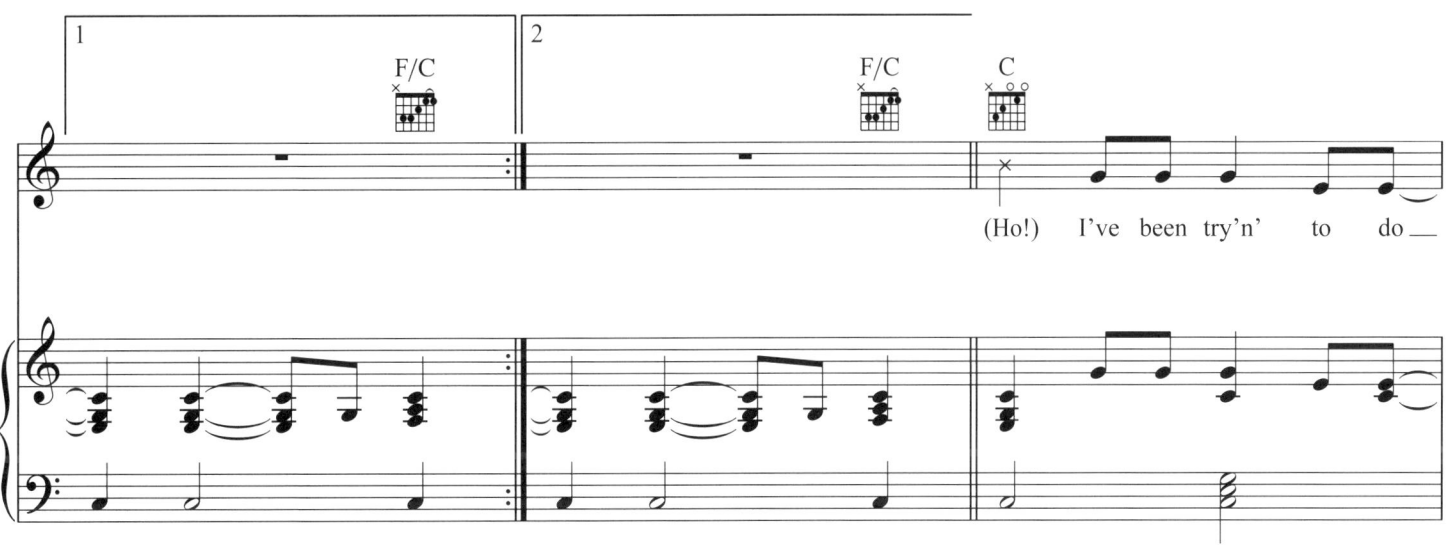

Copyright © 2011 The Lumineers
All Rights Exclusively Administered by Songs Of Kobalt Music Publishing
All Rights Reserved   Used by Permission

FIREWORK

Words and Music by KATY PERRY,
MIKKEL ERIKSEN, TOR ERIK HERMANSEN,
ESTHER DEAN and SANDY WILHELM

© 2010 WHEN I'M RICH YOU'LL BE MY BITCH, EMI MUSIC PUBLISHING LTD., PEERMUSIC III, LTD., DAT DAMN DEAN MUSIC, 2412 LLC and DIPIU SRL
All Rights for WHEN I'M RICH YOU'LL BE MY BITCH Administered by WB MUSIC CORP.
All Rights for EMI MUSIC PUBLISHING LTD. in the U.S. and Canada Controlled and Administered by EMI APRIL MUSIC INC.
All Rights for DAT DAMN DEAN MUSIC and 2412 LLC Controlled and Administered by PEERMUSIC III, LTD.
All Rights for DIPIU SRL Administered by DOWNTOWN DMP SONGS
All Rights Reserved   Used by Permission

FORGET YOU

Words and Music by BRUNO MARS, ARI LEVINE, PHILIP LAWRENCE, THOMAS CALLAWAY and BRODY BROWN

Copyright © 2010 BMG Firefly, Mars Force Music, BMG Gold Songs, Toy Plane Music, Chrysalis Music Ltd., God Given Music, WB Music Corp., Roc Nation Music, Music Famamanem,
Westside Independent Music Publishing LLC, Late 80's Music, Northside Independent Music Publishing LLC, Thou Art The Hunger and Round Hill Songs
All Rights for BMG Firefly, Mars Force Music, BMG Gold Songs, Toy Plane Music, Chrysalis Music Ltd. and God Given Music Administered by BMG Rights Management (US) LLC
All Rights for Roc Nation Music and Music Famamanem Administered by WB Music Corp.
All Rights for Late 80's Music Administered by Westside Independent Music Publishing LLC
All Rights for Thou Art The Hunger Administered by Northside Independent Music Publishing LLC
All Rights Reserved   Used by Permission

GET LUCKY

Words and Music by THOMAS BANGALTER,
GUY MANUEL HOMEM CHRISTO, PHARRELL WILLIAMS
and NILE RODGERS

Copyright © 2013 Imagem CV, EMI April Music Inc., More Water From Nazareth and XLC Music
All Rights for More Water From Nazareth Controlled and Administered by EMI April Music Inc.
All Rights for XLC Music Administered by Sony/ATV Music Publishing LLC, 424 Church Street, Suite 1200, Nashville, TN 37219
All Rights Reserved   Used by Permission

Bm let's ____ raise the bar ____ **D** and our cups ____ **F#m** to the stars. __

E

Bm She's up __ all night _ 'til the sun.

D I'm up __ all night _ to get some. **F#m** She's up __ all night _ for good fun.

E I'm up __ all night _ to get luck-y. **Bm** We're up __ all night _ 'til the sun.

HAPPY
from DESPICABLE ME 2

Words and Music by
PHARRELL WILLIAMS

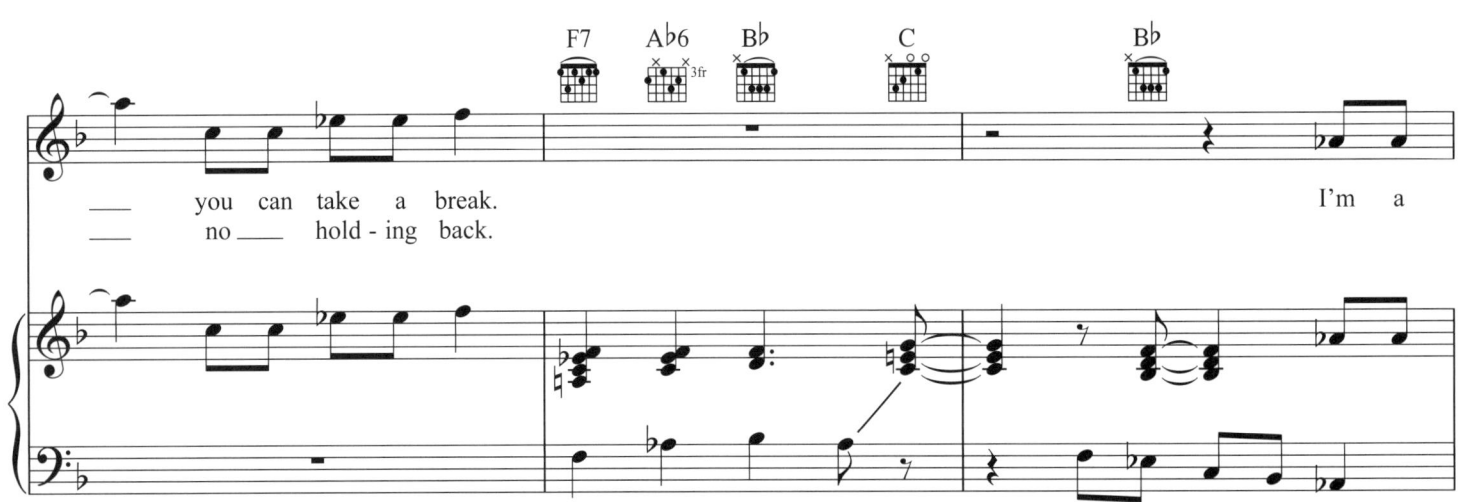

HEY, SOUL SISTER

Words and Music by PAT MONAHAN,
ESPEN LIND and AMUND BJØRKLAND

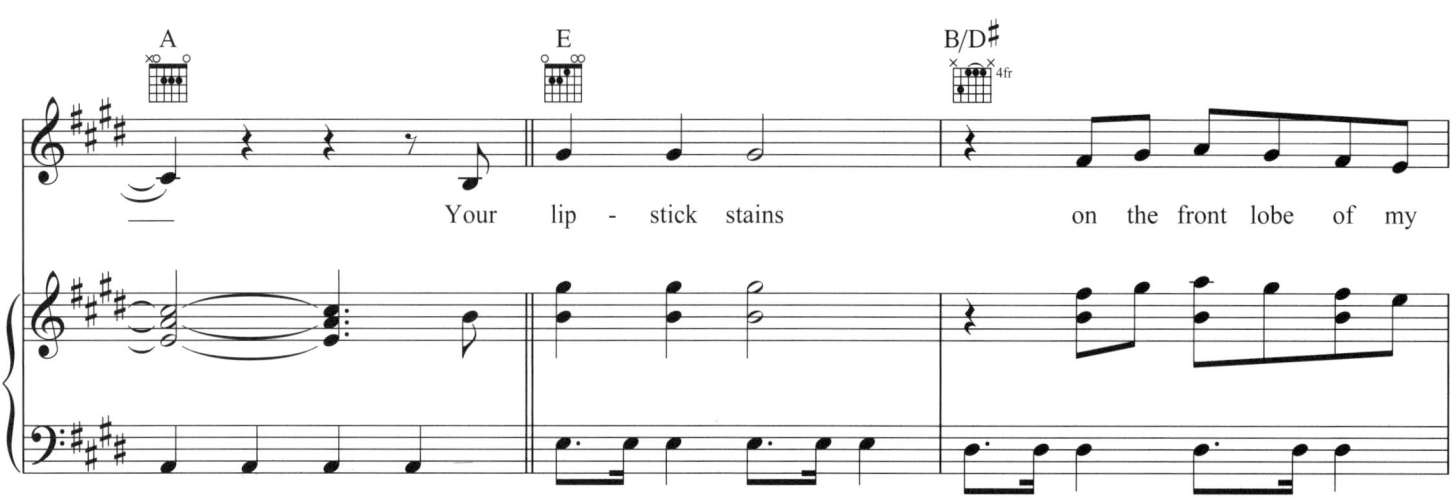

Copyright © 2009 EMI April Music Inc., Blue Lamp Music and Stellar Songs Ltd.
All Rights Administered by Sony/ATV Music Publishing LLC, 424 Church Street, Suite 1200, Nashville, TN 37219
International Copyright Secured   All Rights Reserved

HOME

Words and Music by GREG HOLDEN
and DREW PEARSON

THE HOUSE THAT BUILT ME

Words and Music by TOM DOUGLAS
and ALLEN SHAMBLIN

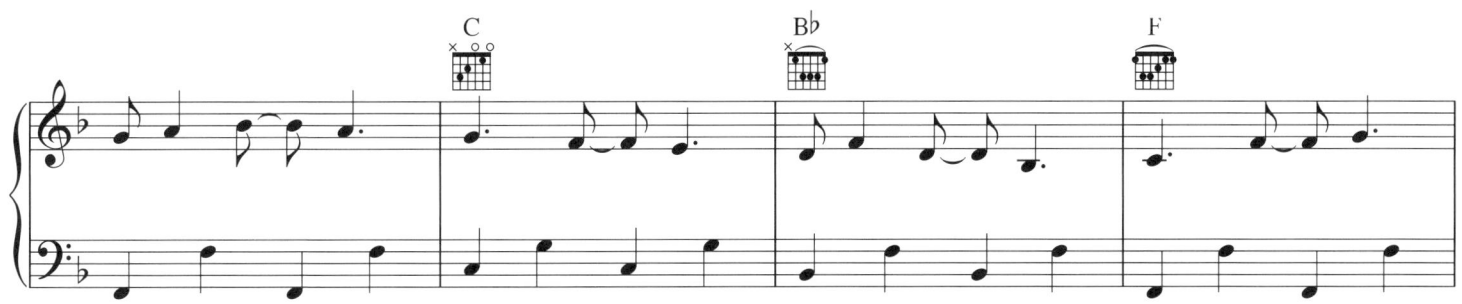

Copyright © 2009 Sony/ATV Music Publishing LLC, Tomdouglasmusic and Built On Rock Music
All Rights on behalf of Sony/ATV Music Publishing LLC and Tomdouglasmusic Administered by Sony/ATV Music Publishing LLC, 424 Church Street, Suite 1200, Nashville, TN 37219
All Rights on behalf of Built On Rock Music Administered by ClearBox Rights
International Copyright Secured   All Rights Reserved

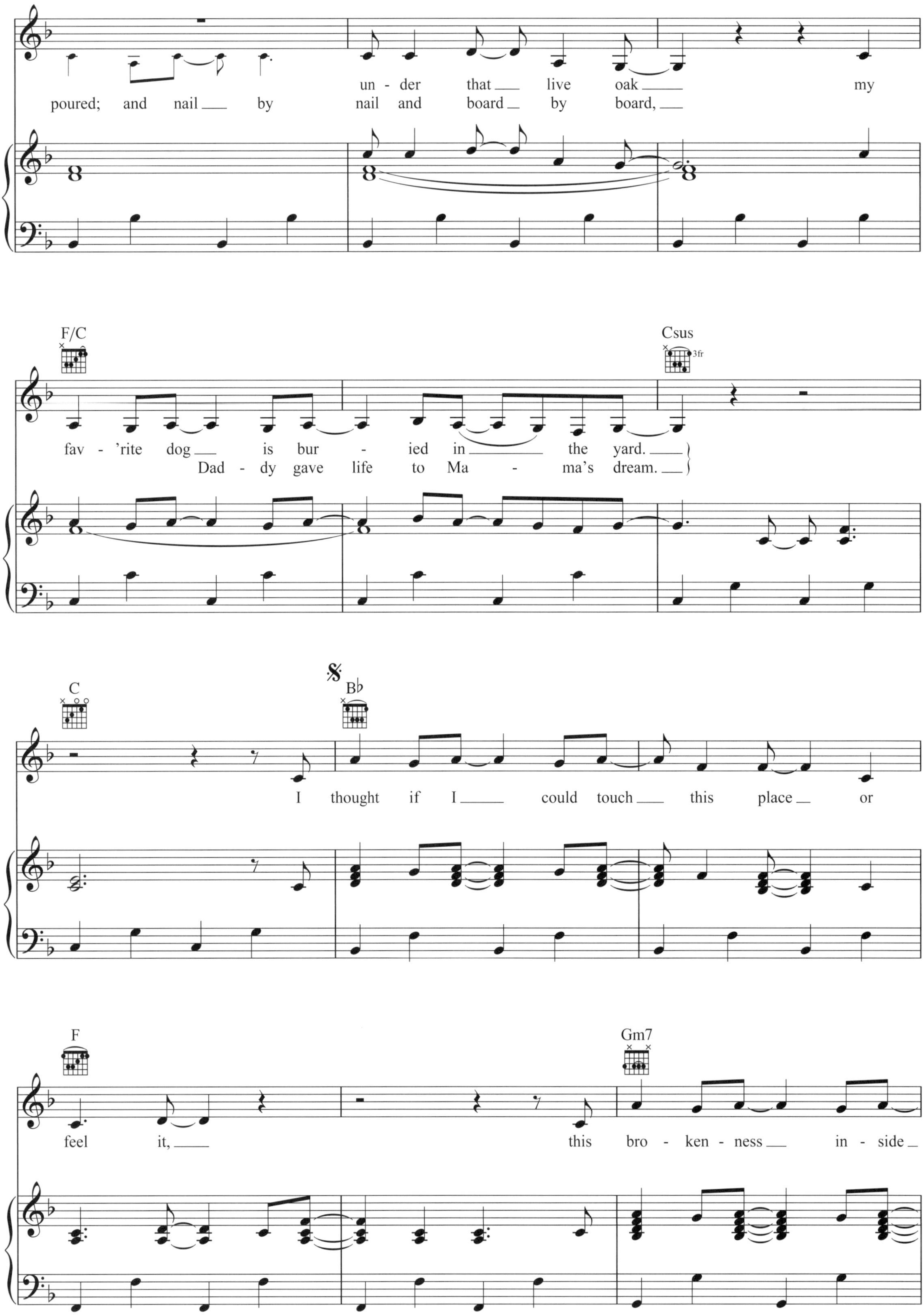
un - der that live oak my
poured; and nail by nail and board by board,
F/C
Csus
3fr
fav - 'rite dog is bur - ied in the yard.
Dad - dy gave life to Ma - ma's dream.
C
B♭
I thought if I could touch this place or
F
Gm7
feel it, this bro - ken - ness in - side

I KNEW YOU WERE TROUBLE

Words and Music by TAYLOR SWIFT,
SHELLBACK and MAX MARTIN

Once up-on a time, a
No a-pol-o-gies, he'll

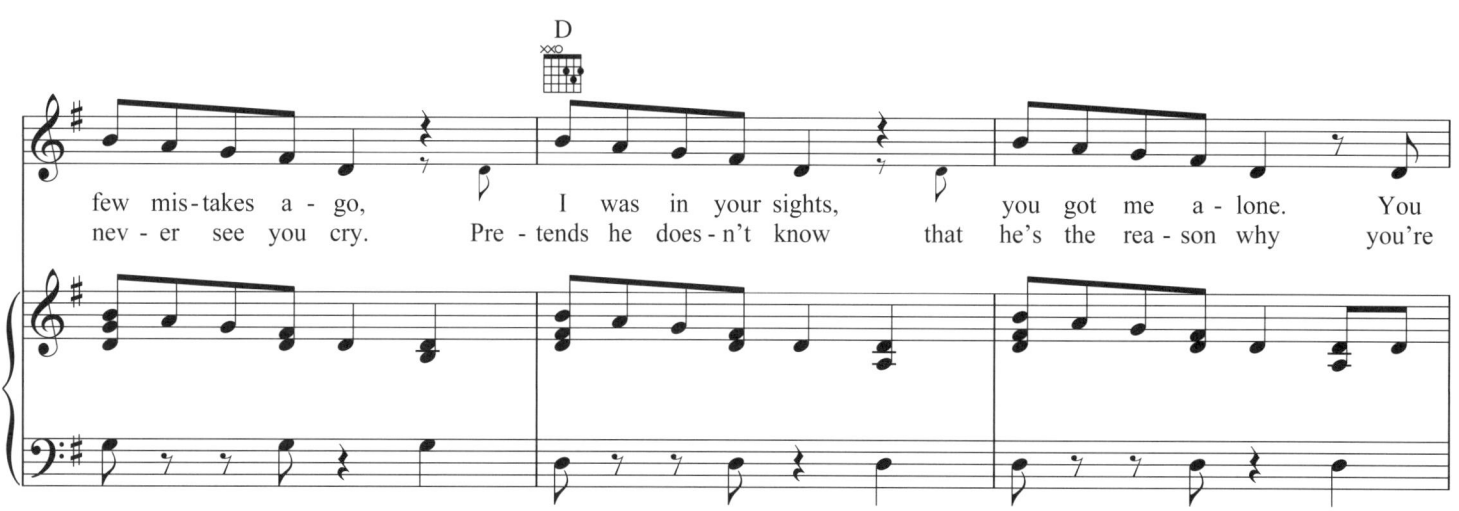

few mis-takes a-go, I was in your sights, you got me a-lone. You
nev-er see you cry. Pre-tends he does-n't know that he's the rea-son why you're

found ___ me, you found ___ me, you found ___ me, ee,
drown-ing, you're drown-ing, you're drown-ing, ing,

Copyright © 2012 Sony/ATV Music Publishing LLC, Taylor Swift Music and MXM Music AB
All Rights on behalf of Sony/ATV Music Publishing LLC and Taylor Swift Music Administered by Sony/ATV Music Publishing LLC, 424 Church Street, Suite 1200, Nashville, TN 37219
All Rights of MXM Music AB Exclusively Administered by Kobalt Songs Music Publishing
International Copyright Secured All Rights Reserved

I WILL WAIT

Words and Music by
MUMFORD & SONS

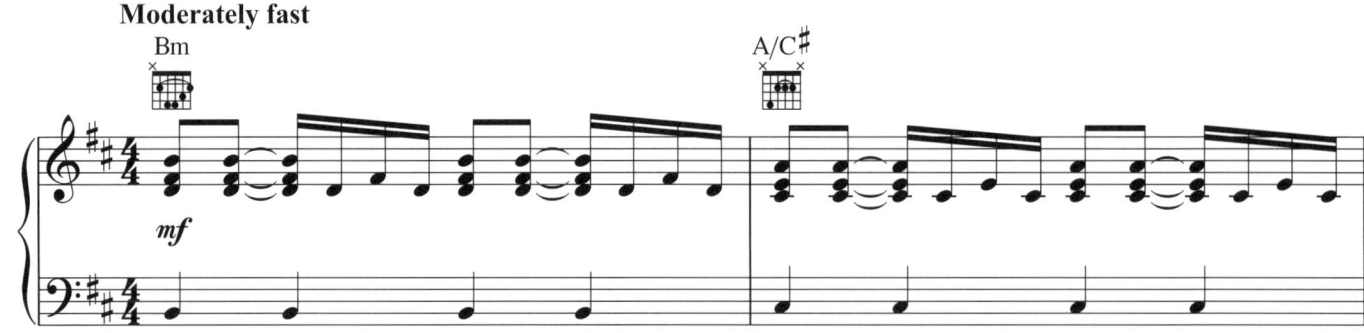

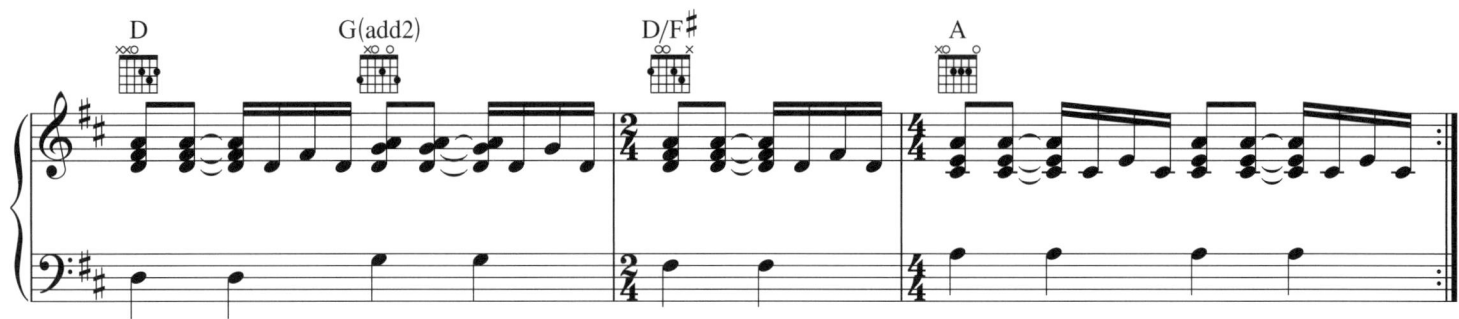

Well, I came home
dust

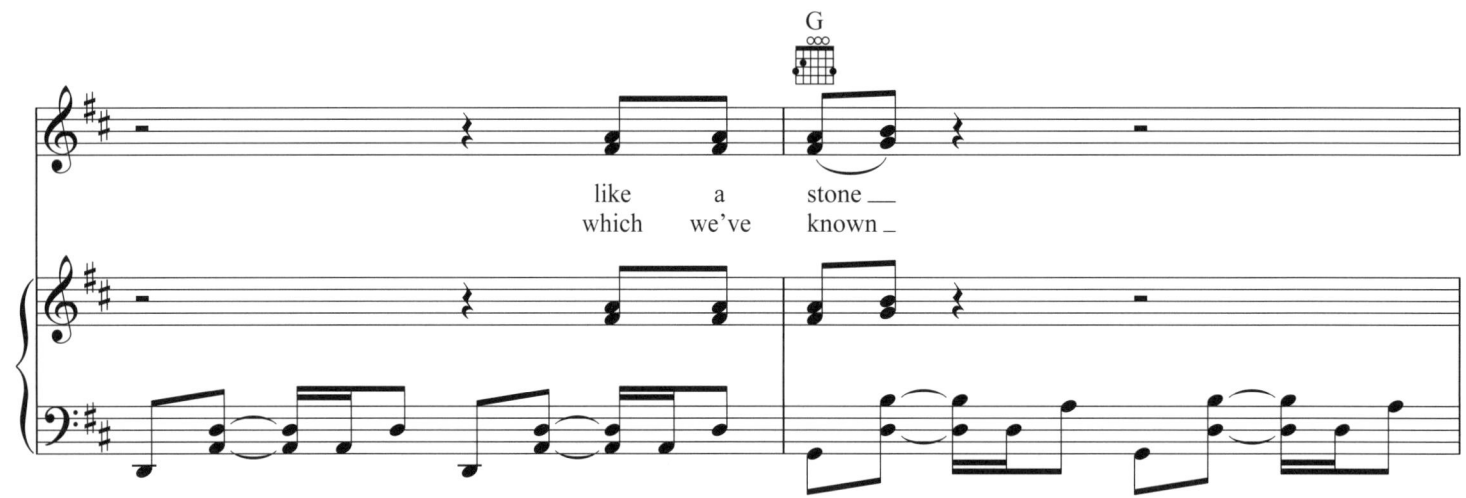

like a stone
which we've known

Copyright © 2012 UNIVERSAL MUSIC PUBLISHING LTD.
All Rights in the U.S. and Canada Controlled and Administered by UNIVERSAL - POLYGRAM INTERNATIONAL TUNES, INC.
All Rights Reserved   Used by Permission

194

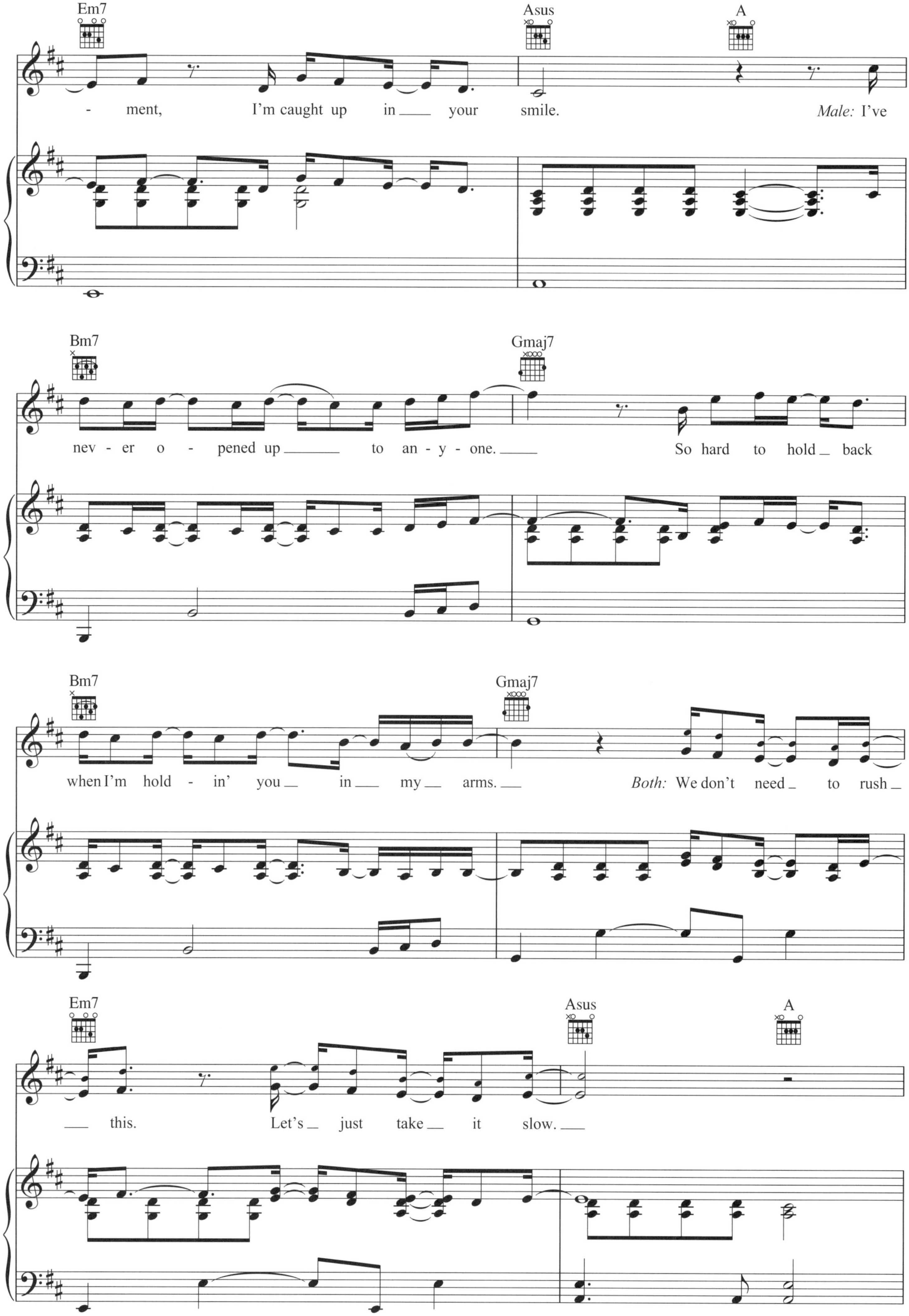
Em7
Asus
A
-ment, I'm caught up in your smile. Male: I've
Bm7
Gmaj7
nev - er o - pened up to an - y - one. So hard to hold back
Bm7
Gmaj7
when I'm hold - in' you in my arms. Both: We don't need to rush
Em7
Asus
A
this. Let's just take it slow.

I WON'T GIVE UP

Words and Music by JASON MRAZ
and MICHAEL NATTER

*Guitarists: Tune 6th string down to D.

Copyright © 2012 Goo Eyed Music (ASCAP) and Great Hooks Music c/o No BS Publishing (ASCAP)
International Copyright Secured   All Rights Reserved

JAR OF HEARTS

Words and Music by BARRETT YERETSIAN,
CHRISTINA PERRI and DREW LAWRENCE

Copyright © 2010, 2011 BMG Rights Management (UK) Ltd., Philosophy Of Sound Publishing, Miss Perri Lane Publishing, WB Music Corp. and Piggy Dog Music
All Rights for BMG Rights Management (UK) Ltd. and Philosophy Of Sound Publishing Administered by BMG Rights Management (US) LLC
All Rights for Miss Perri Lane Publishing Administered by Songs Of Kobalt Music Publishing
All Rights for Piggy Dog Music Administered by WB Music Corp.
All Rights Reserved   Used by Permission

JUST GIVE ME A REASON

Words and Music by ALECIA MOORE,
JEFF BHASKER and NATE RUESS

JUST THE WAY YOU ARE

Words and Music by BRUNO MARS,
ARI LEVINE, PHILIP LAWRENCE,
KHARI CAIN and KHALIL WALTON

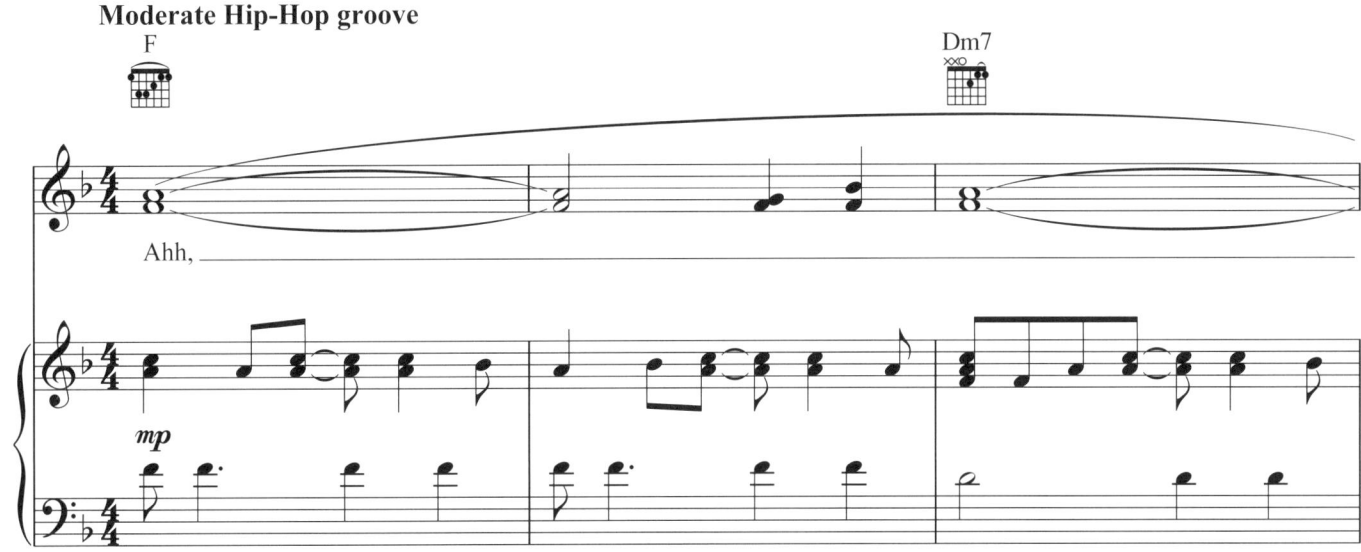

© 2009, 2010 BMG FIREFLY, MARSFORCE MUSIC, BMG GOLD SONGS, TOY PLANE MUSIC, ROUND HILL SONGS, WB MUSIC CORP., UPPER DEC,
ROC NATION MUSIC, MUSIC FAMAMANEM, NORTHSIDE INDEPENDENT MUSIC PUBLISHING LLC, UNIVERSAL MUSIC CORP. and DRY RAIN ENTERTAINMENT
All Rights for BMG FIREFLY, MARSFORCE MUSIC, BMG GOLD SONGS and TOY PLANE MUSIC Administered by BMG RIGHTS MANAGEMENT (US) LLC
All Rights for UPPER DEC, ROC NATION MUSIC and MUSIC FAMAMANEM Administered by WB MUSIC CORP.
All Rights for DRY RAIN ENTERTAINMENT Controlled and Administered by UNIVERSAL MUSIC CORP.
All Rights Reserved   Used by Permission

LAY ME DOWN

Words and Music by SAM SMITH,
JAMES NAPIER and ELVIN SMITH

Copyright © 2014 Sony/ATV Music Publishing Limited UK, Naughty Words Limited, Stellar Songs Ltd. and Salli Isaak Songs Ltd.
All Rights on behalf of Sony/ATV Music Publishing Limited UK, Naughty Words Limited and Stellar Songs Ltd. Administered by
Sony/ATV Music Publishing LLC, 424 Church Street, Suite 1200, Nashville, TN 37219
All Rights on behalf of Salli Isaak Songs Ltd. in the U.S. and Canada Administered by Universal - PolyGram International Tunes, Inc.
International Copyright Secured All Rights Reserved

237

LET IT GO
from Disney's Animated Feature FROZEN

Music and Lyrics by KRISTEN ANDERSON-LOPEZ
and ROBERT LOPEZ

MEAN

Words and Music by
TAYLOR SWIFT

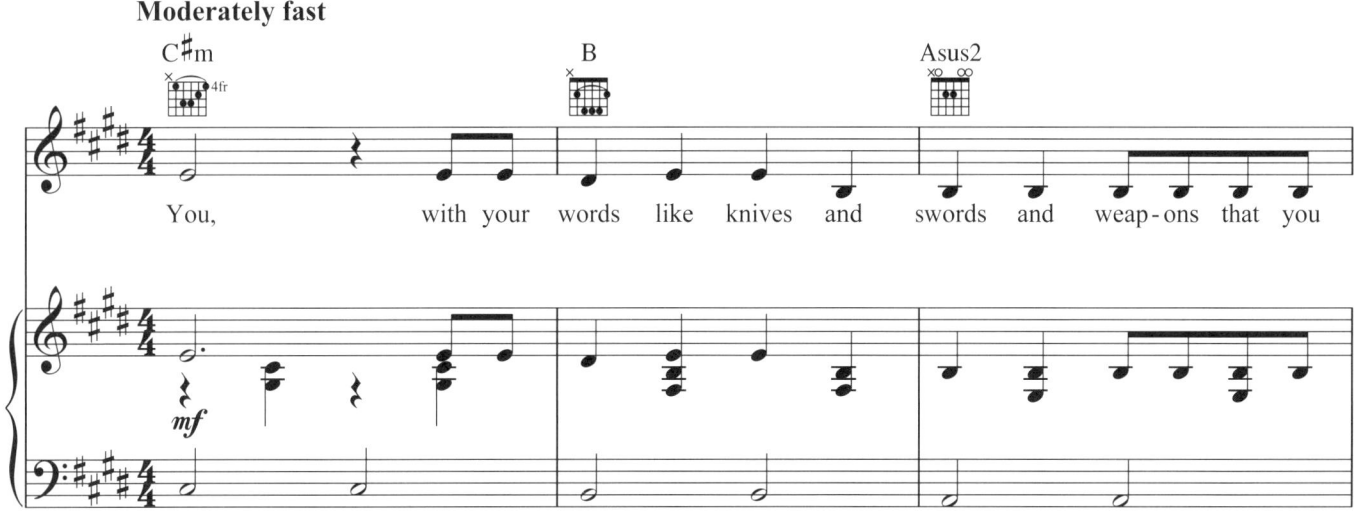
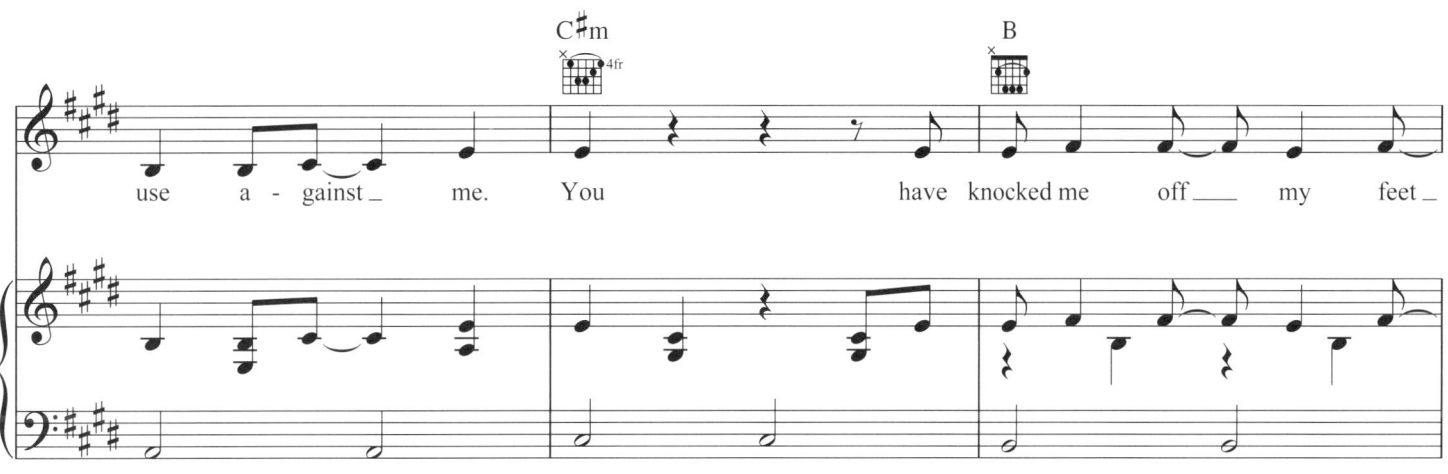

Copyright © 2010 Sony/ATV Music Publishing LLC and Taylor Swift Music
All Rights Administered by Sony/ATV Music Publishing LLC, 424 Church Street, Suite 1200, Nashville, TN 37219
International Copyright Secured   All Rights Reserved

LITTLE TALKS

Words and Music by
OF MONSTERS AND MEN

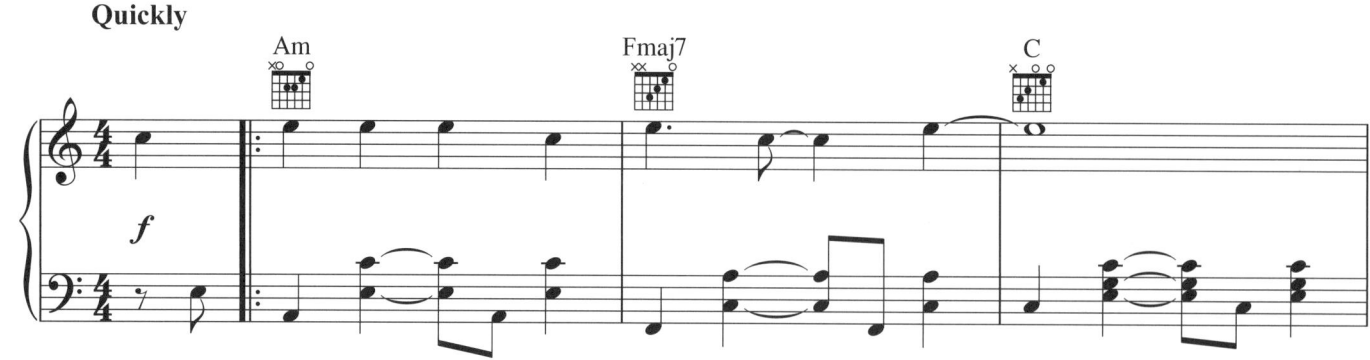
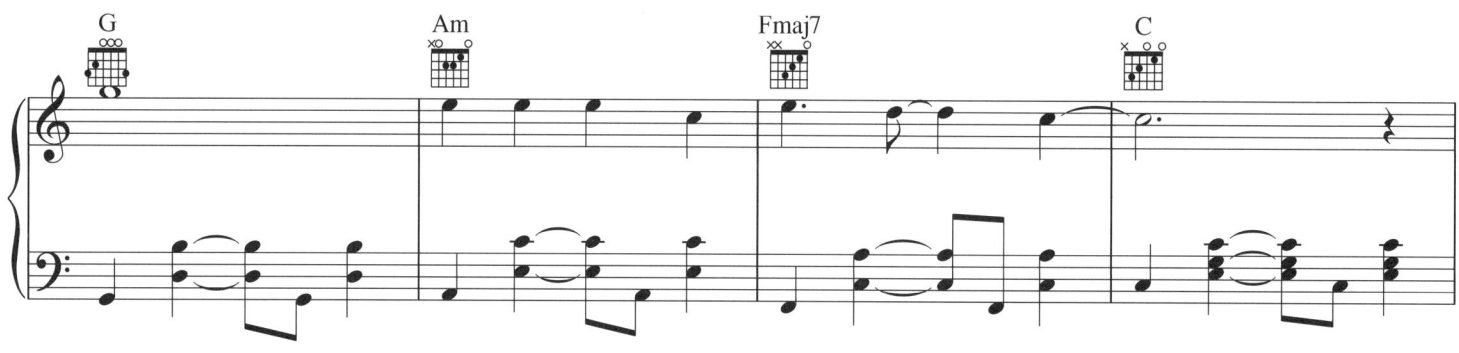
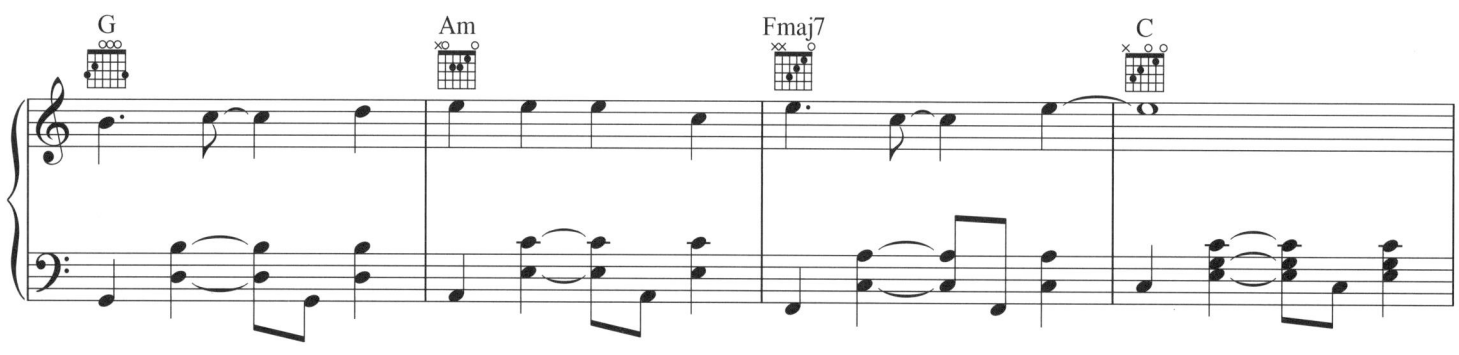
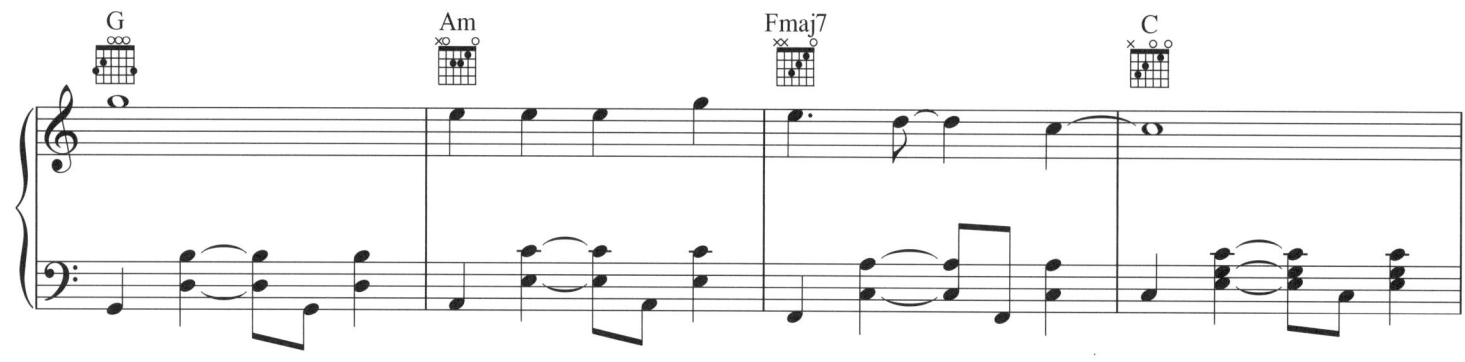

Copyright © 2012 Sony/ATV Music Publishing LLC, NannBH Music and Mussi Music
All Rights Administered by Sony/ATV Music Publishing LLC, 424 Church Street, Suite 1200, Nashville, TN 37219
International Copyright Secured   All Rights Reserved

sound the same. Though the truth may vary, this ship will carry our bodies safe to shore.

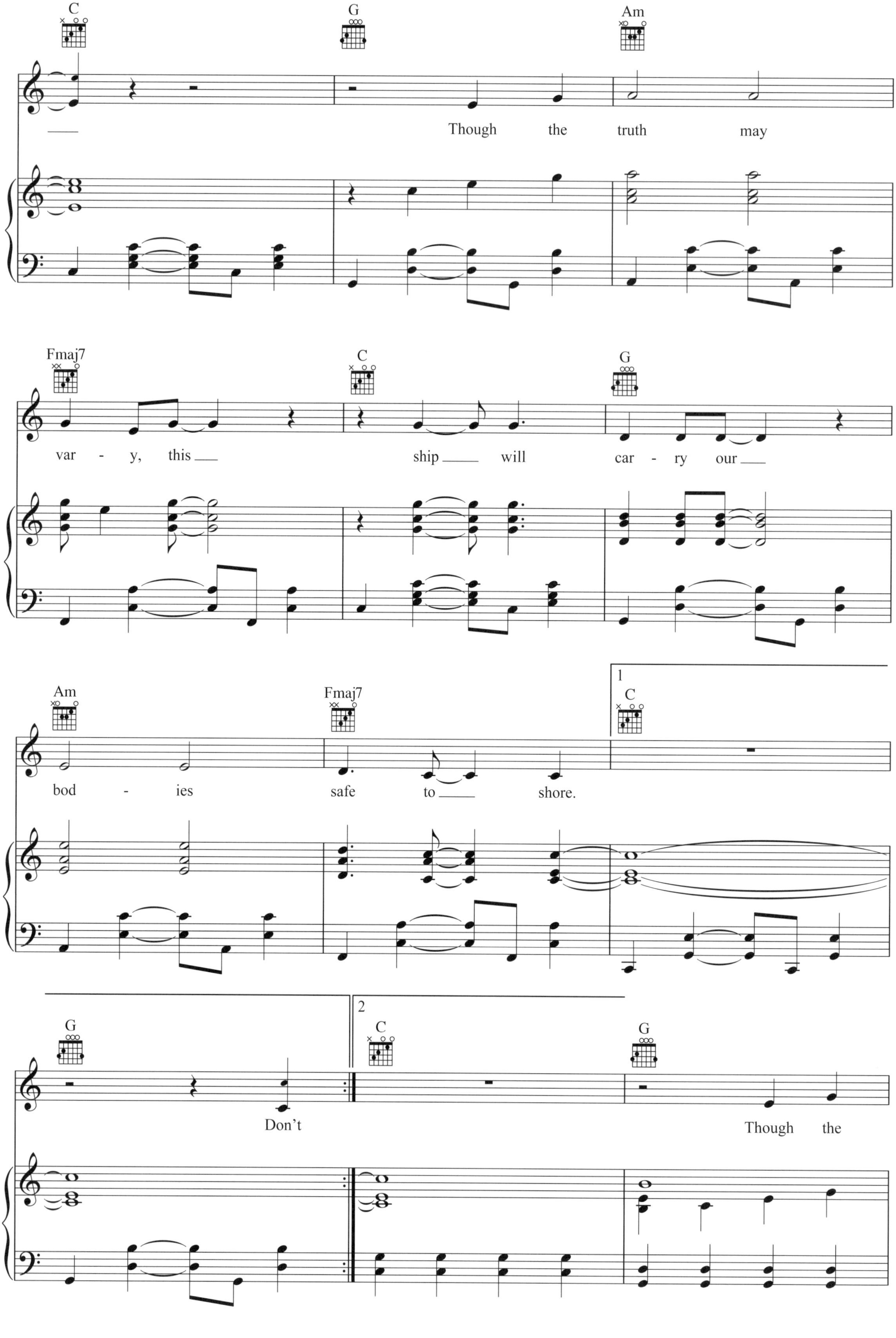

C
G
Am
Though the truth may
Fmaj7
C
G
var - y, this ship will car - ry our
Am
Fmaj7
1
C
bod - ies safe to shore.
G
2
C
G
Don't
Though the

MOVES LIKE JAGGER

Words and Music by ADAM LEVINE,
BENJAMIN LEVIN, AMMAR MALIK
and JOHAN SCHUSTER

Copyright © 2010, 2011 by Universal Music - Careers, Sudgee Music, Matza Ball Music, Where Da Kasz At?, Lotzah Balls Soup, Prescription Songs, Maru Cha Cha and MXM Music AB
All Rights for Sudgee Music Administered by Universal Music - Careers
All Rights for Matza Ball Music Administered by Songs Of Universal, Inc.
All Rights for Where Da Kasz At?, Lotzah Balls Soup, Prescription Songs, Maru Cha Cha and MXM Music AB Administered by Kobalt Music Publishing America, Inc.
International Copyright Secured All Rights Reserved

RADIOACTIVE

Words and Music by DANIEL REYNOLDS,
BENJAMIN McKEE, DANIEL SERMON,
ALEXANDER GRANT and JOSH MOSSER

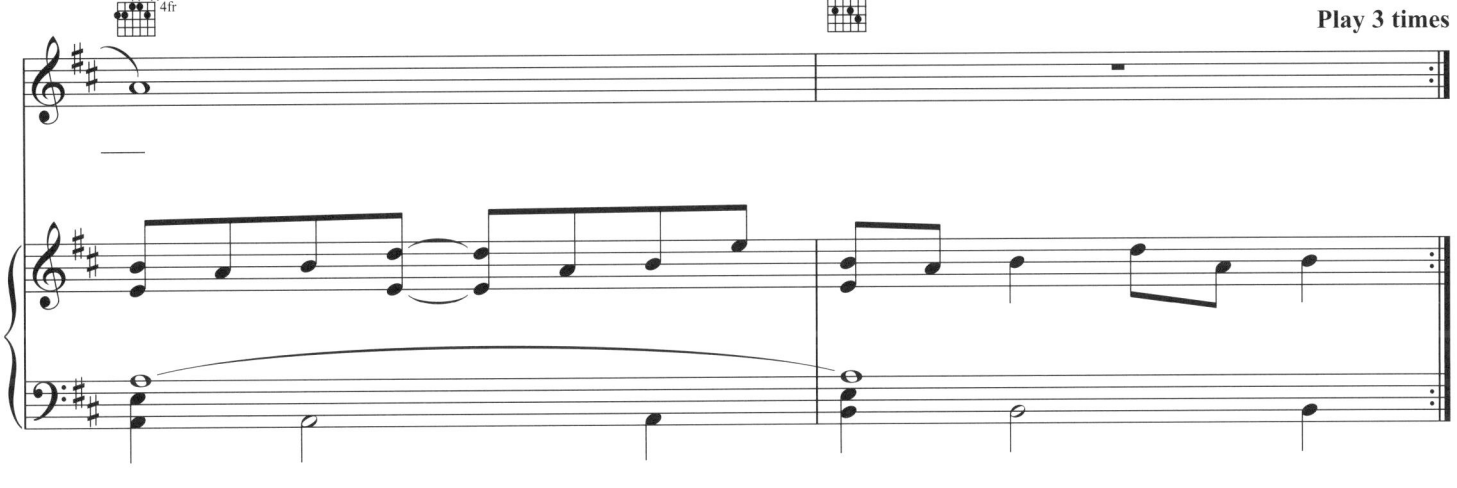

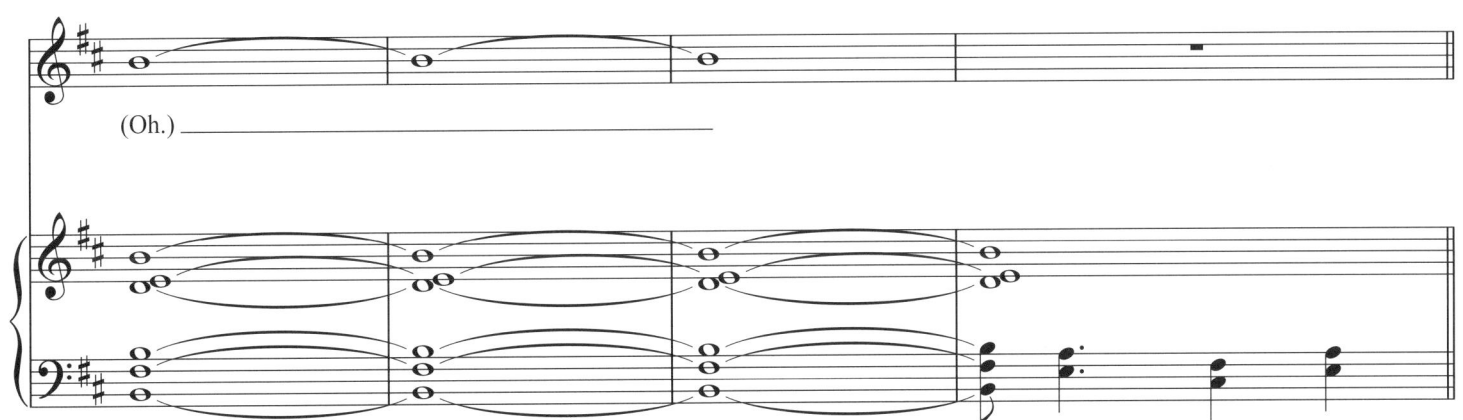

Copyright © 2012 SONGS OF UNIVERSAL, INC., IMAGINE DRAGONS PUBLISHING, ALEXANDER GRANT and JMOSSER MUSIC
All Rights for IMAGINE DRAGONS PUBLISHING and ALEXANDER GRANT Controlled and Administered by SONGS OF UNIVERSAL, INC.
All Rights Reserved   Used by Permission

POMPEII

Words and Music by
DAN SMITH

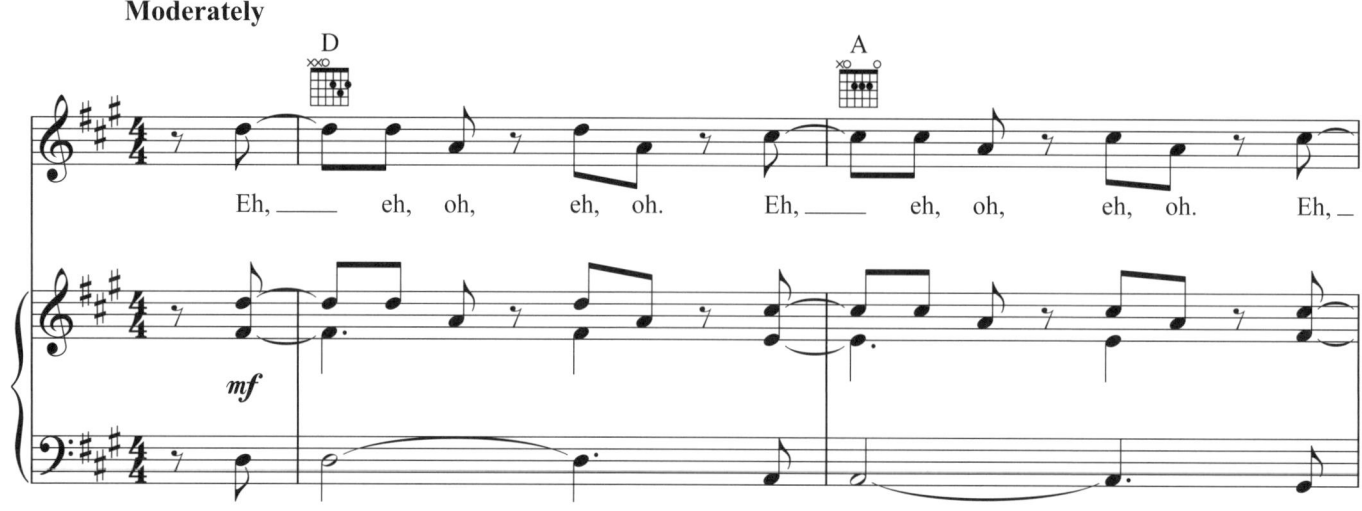

Copyright © 2013 BASTILLE MUSIC LTD.
All Rights in the U.S. and Canada Controlled and Administered by UNIVERSAL - POLYGRAM INTERNATIONAL PUBLISHING, INC.
All Rights Reserved   Used by Permission

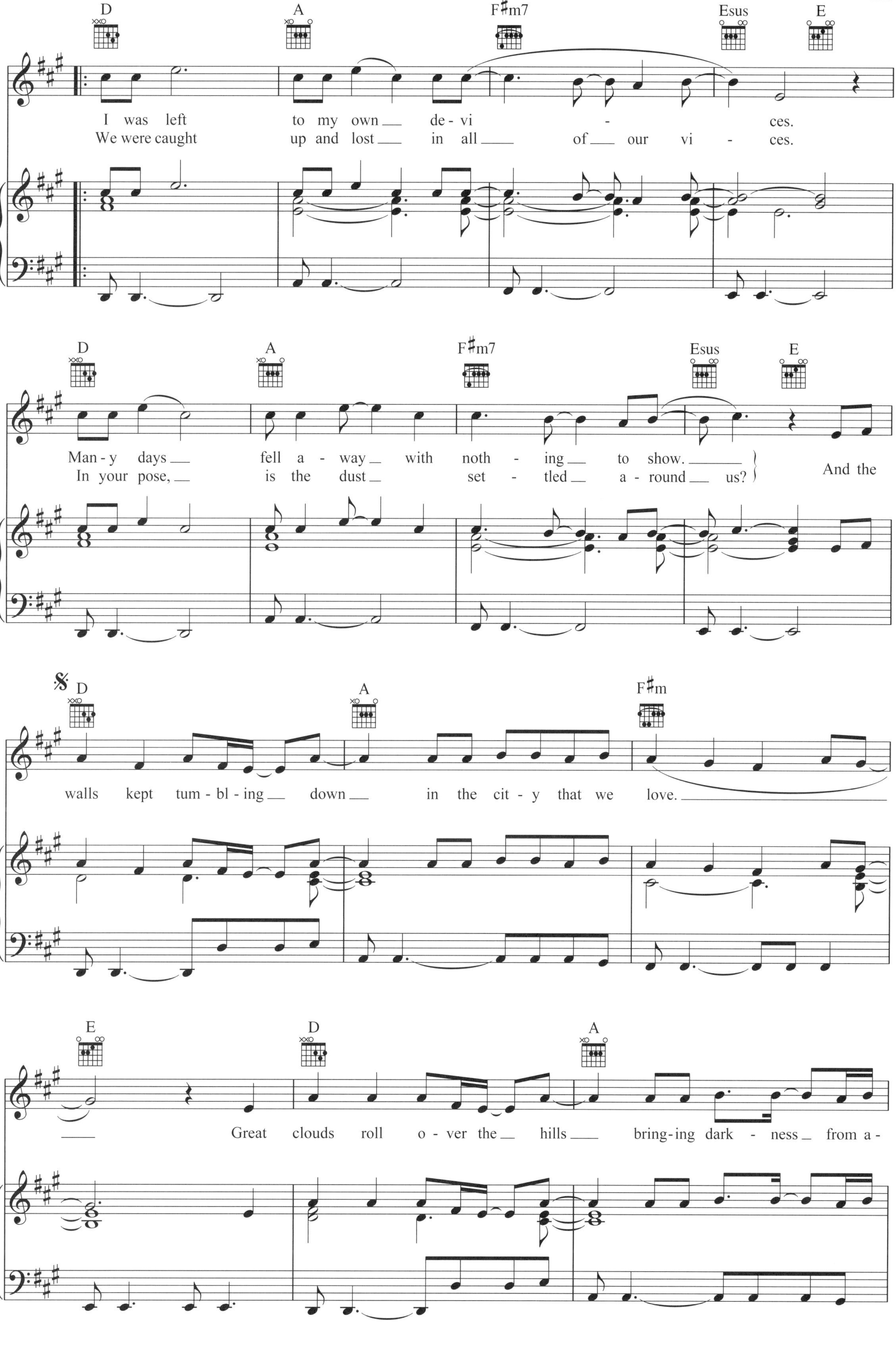
D A F♯m7 Esus E
I was left to my own de-vi - ces.
We were caught up and lost in all of our vi - ces.
D A F♯m7 Esus E
Man-y days fell a-way with noth - ing to show.
In your pose, is the dust set - tled a-round us?
And the
D A F♯m
walls kept tum-bl-ing down in the cit-y that we love.
E D A
Great clouds roll o-ver the hills bring-ing dark - ness from a -

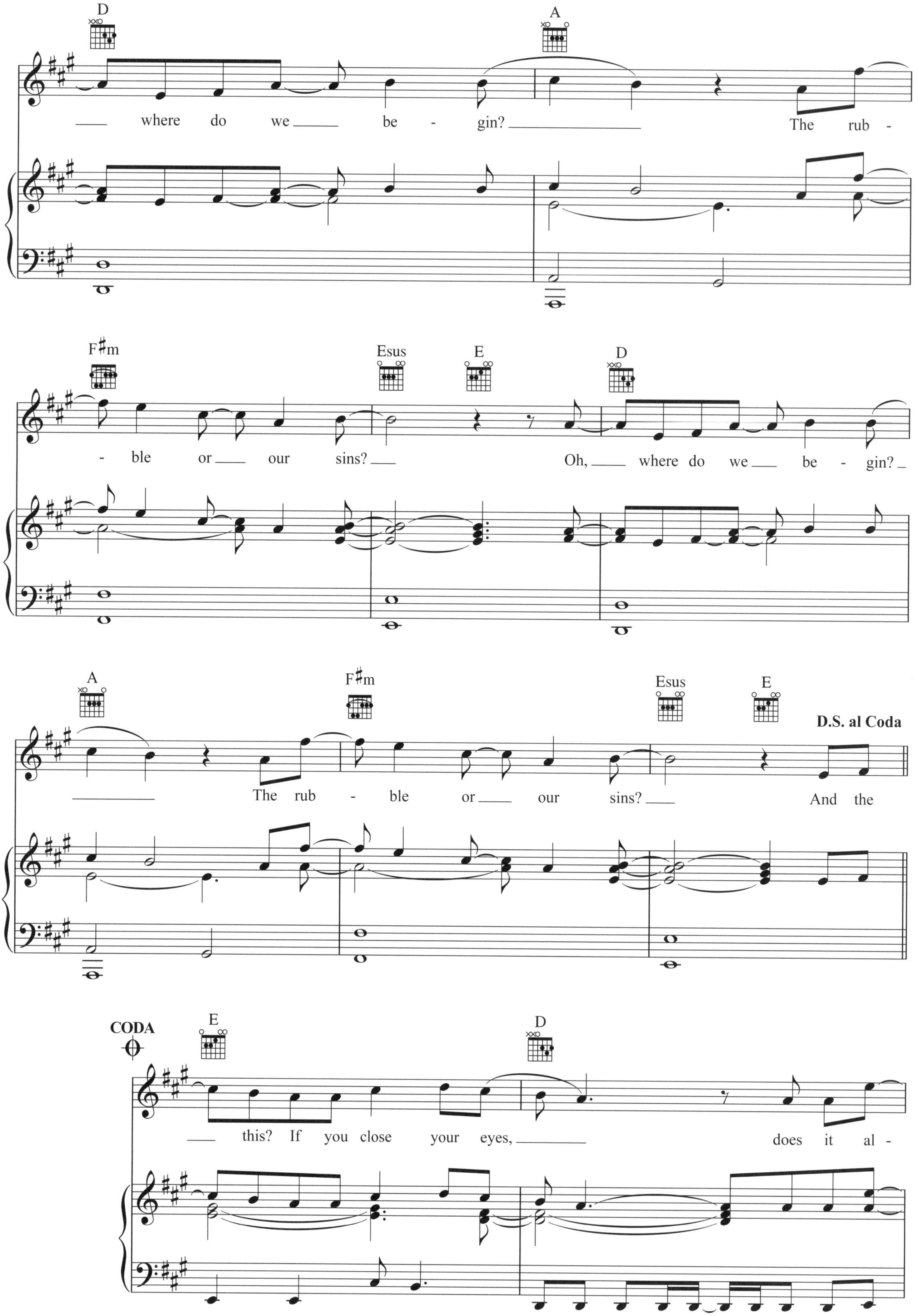
D
A
where do we be - gin?
The rub -
F♯m
Esus
E
D
- ble or our sins?
Oh, where do we be - gin?
A
F♯m
Esus
E
D.S. al Coda
The rub - ble or our sins?
And the
CODA
E
D
this? If you close your eyes,
does it al -

Rap: *(See additional lyrics)*

Additional Lyrics

Rap: Smart money bettin' I'll be better off without you.
In no time I'll be forgettin' all about you.
You sayin' that you know, but I really, really doubt it.
You understand? My life is easy when I ain't around you.
Iggy, Iggy too biggie to be here stressin'.
I'm thinkin' I love the thought of you more than I love your presence.
And the best thing now is probably for you to exit.
I let you go, let you back. I finally learned my lesson.
No half-steppin', either you want it or you just playin.'
I'm listenin' to you knowin' I can't believe what you're sayin'.
There's a million you's, baby boo, so don't be dumb.
(I got 99 problems but you won't be one, like what?)

ROAR

Words and Music by KATY PERRY, LUKASZ GOTTWALD, MAX MARTIN, BONNIE McKEE and HENRY WALTER

© 2013 WB MUSIC CORP., WHEN I'M RICH YOU'LL BE MY BITCH, SONGS OF PULSE RECORDING, PRESCRIPTION SONGS,
BONNIE McKEE MUSIC, WHERE DA KASZ AT?, MXM MUSIC AB, KASZ MONEY PUBLISHING and ONEIROLOGY PUBLISHING
All Rights for WHEN I'M RICH YOU'LL BE MY BITCH Administered by WB MUSIC CORP.
All Rights for PRESCRIPTION SONGS, MXM MUSIC AB, KASZ MONEY PUBLISHING and ONEIROLOGY PUBLISHING
Administered by KOBALT SONGS MUSIC PUBLISHING
All Rights for BONNIE McKEE MUSIC and WHERE DA KASZ AT? Administered by SONGS OF KOBALT MUSIC PUBLISHING
All Rights Reserved   Used by Permission

ROLLING IN THE DEEP

Words and Music by ADELE ADKINS
and PAUL EPWORTH

318

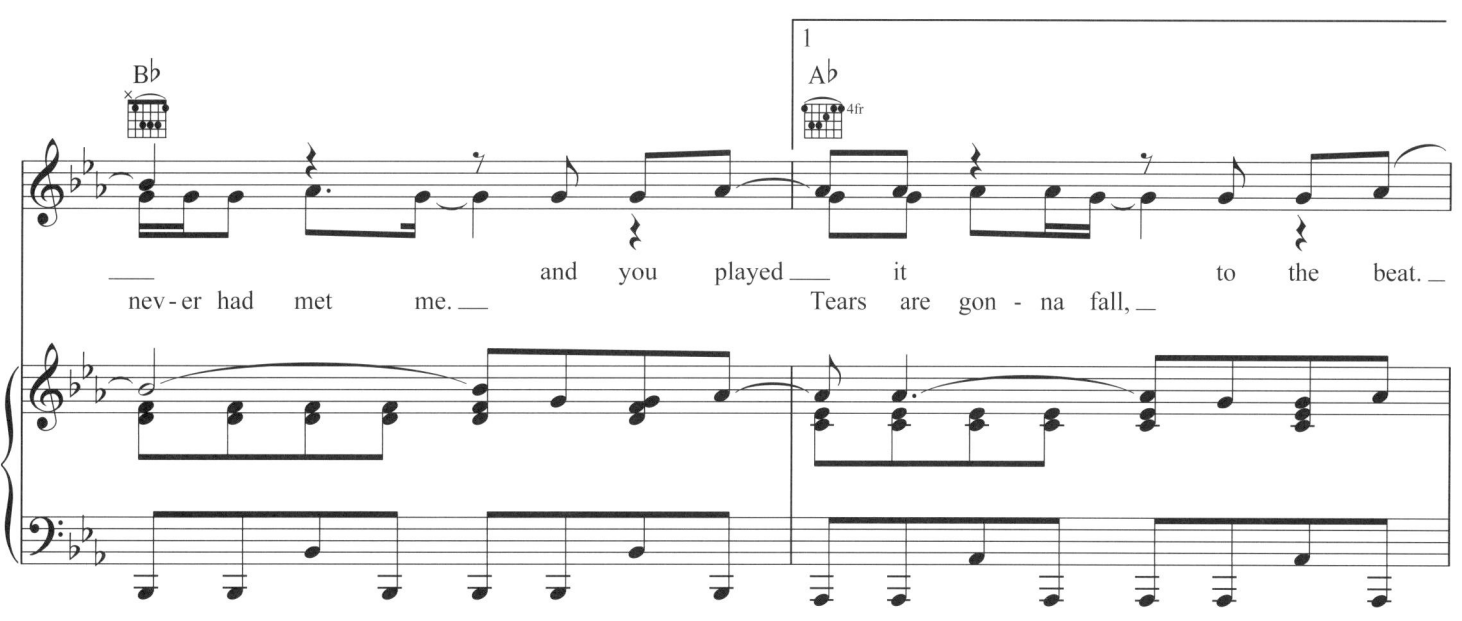
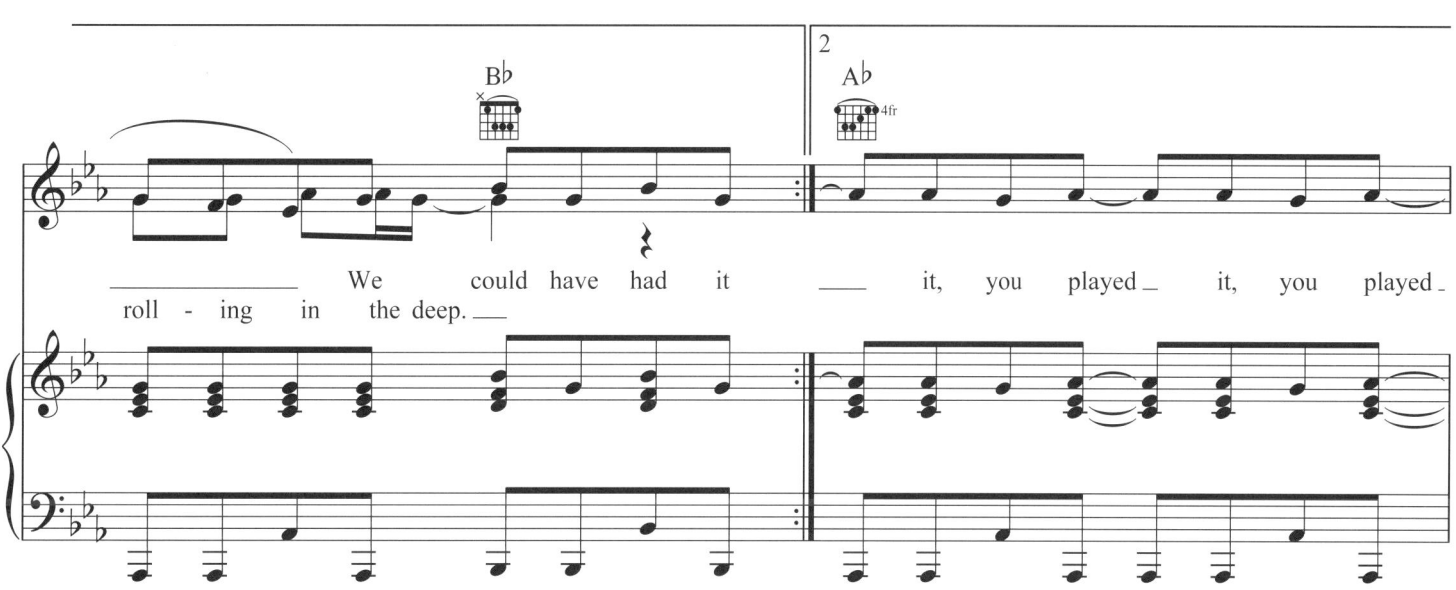
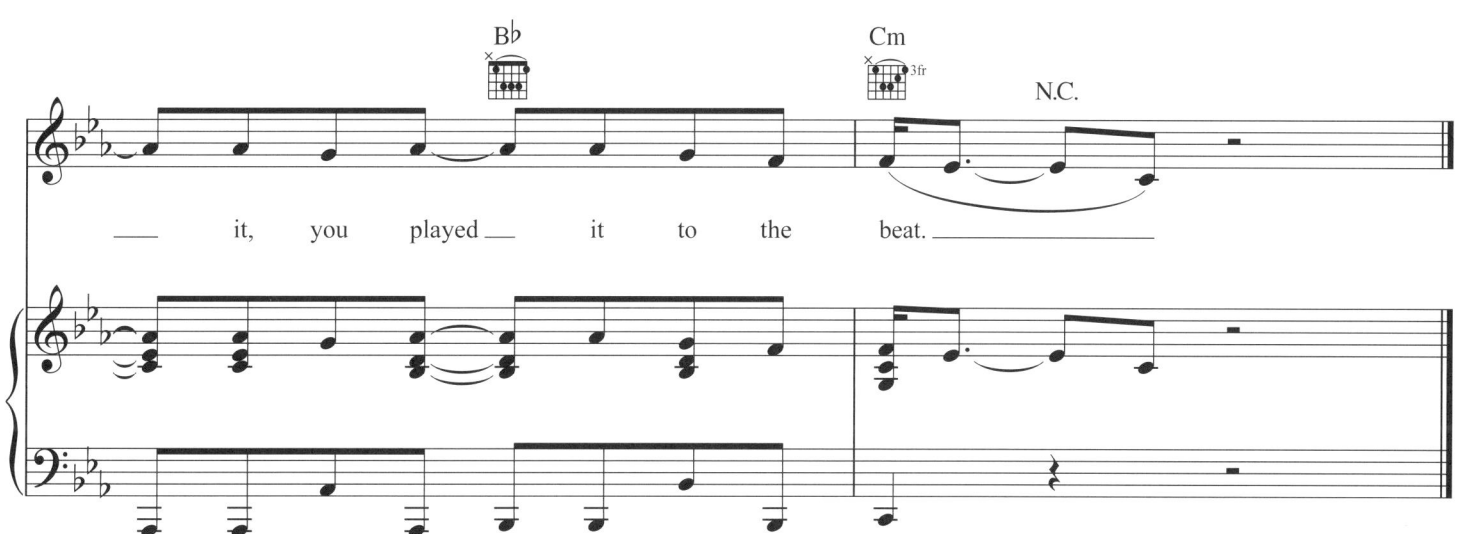

ROYALS

Words and Music by ELLA YELICH-O'CONNOR
and JOEL LITTLE

Moderately

I've nev-er seen a dia-mond in the flesh.
I, we've cracked the code.

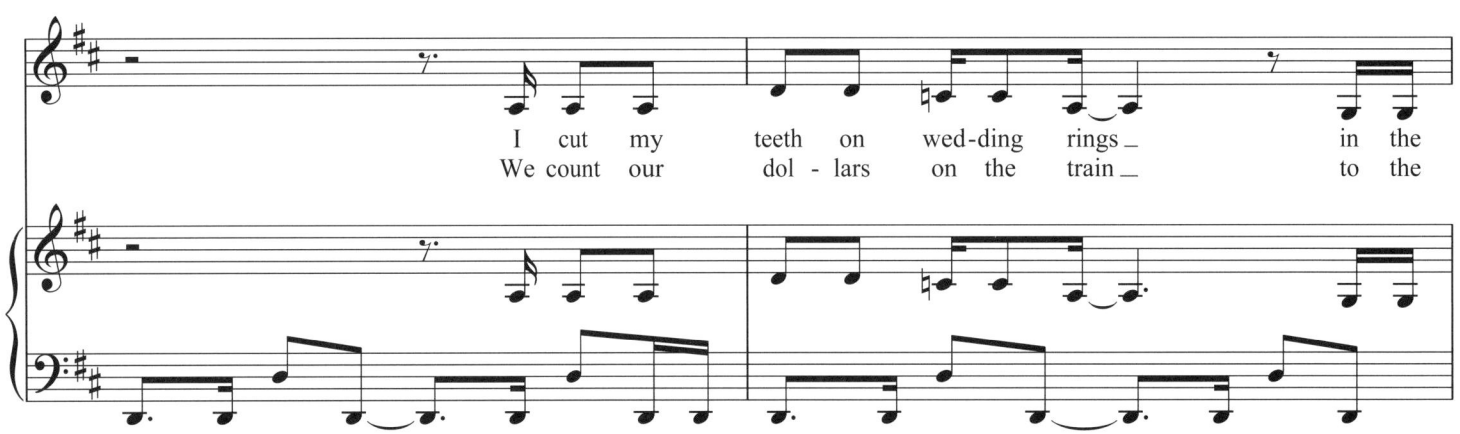

I cut my teeth on wed-ding rings in the
We count our dol-lars on the train to the

mov-ies. And I'm not proud of my ad-dress.
par-ty. And ev-'ry-one who knows us knows

Copyright © 2013 Songs Music Publishing, LLC o/b/o Songs Of SMP and EMI Music Publishing Australia Pty Ltd
All Rights on behalf of EMI Music Publishing Australia Pty Ltd Administered by Sony/ATV Music Publishing LLC, 424 Church Street, Suite 1200, Nashville, TN 37219
All Rights Reserved Used by Permission

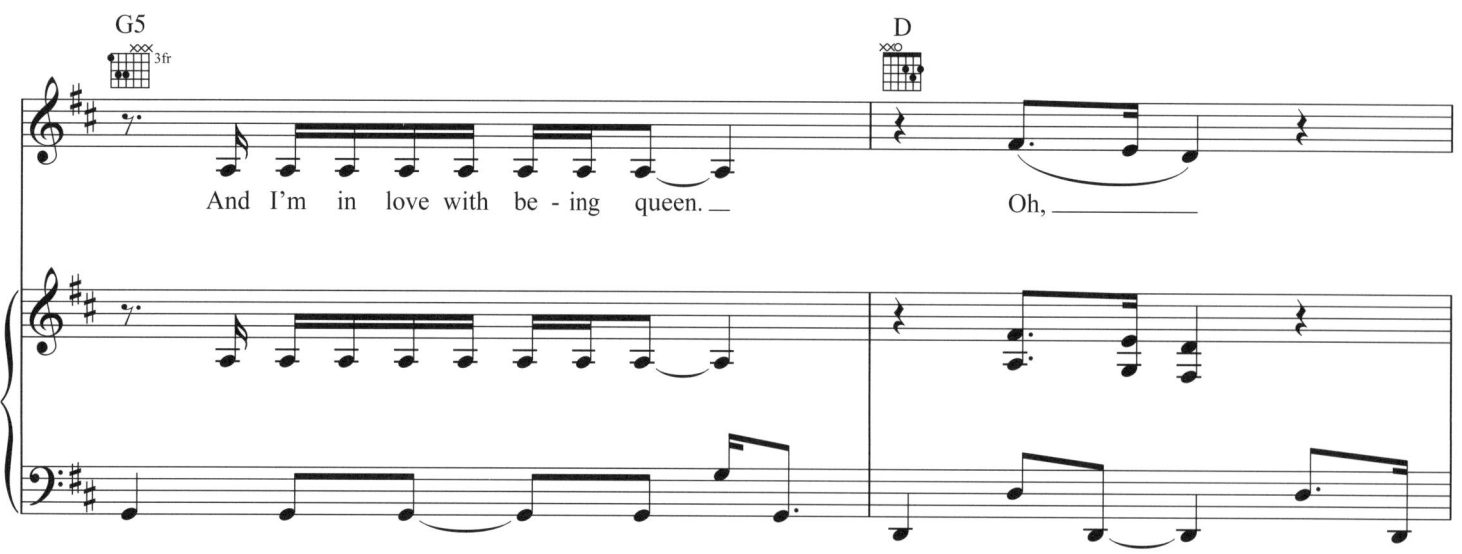

SAY SOMETHING

Words and Music by IAN AXEL, CHAD VACCARINO and MIKE CAMPBELL

SECRETS

SHAKE IT OFF

Words and Music by TAYLOR SWIFT,
MAX MARTIN and SHELLBACK

Copyright © 2014 Sony/ATV Music Publishing LLC, Taylor Swift Music and MXM
All Rights on behalf of Sony/ATV Music Publishing LLC and Taylor Swift Music Administered by Sony/ATV Music Publishing LLC, 424 Church Street, Suite 1200, Nashville, TN 37219
All Rights on behalf of MXM Administered Worldwide by Kobalt Songs Music Publishing
International Copyright Secured All Rights Reserved

Additional Lyrics

Spoken: Hey, hey, hey! Just think: While you've been getting
Down and out about the liars and the dirty, dirty
Cheats of the world, you could've been getting down to
This. Sick. Beat!

Rap: My ex-man brought his new girlfriend.
She's like, "Oh, my god!" But I'm just gonna shake.
And to the fella over there with the hella good hair,
Won't you come on over, baby? We can shake, shake, shake.

SHUT UP AND DANCE

Words and Music by RYAN McMAHON,
BEN BERGER, SEAN WAUGAMAN,
ELI MAIMAN, NICHOLAS PETRICCA
and KEVIN RAY

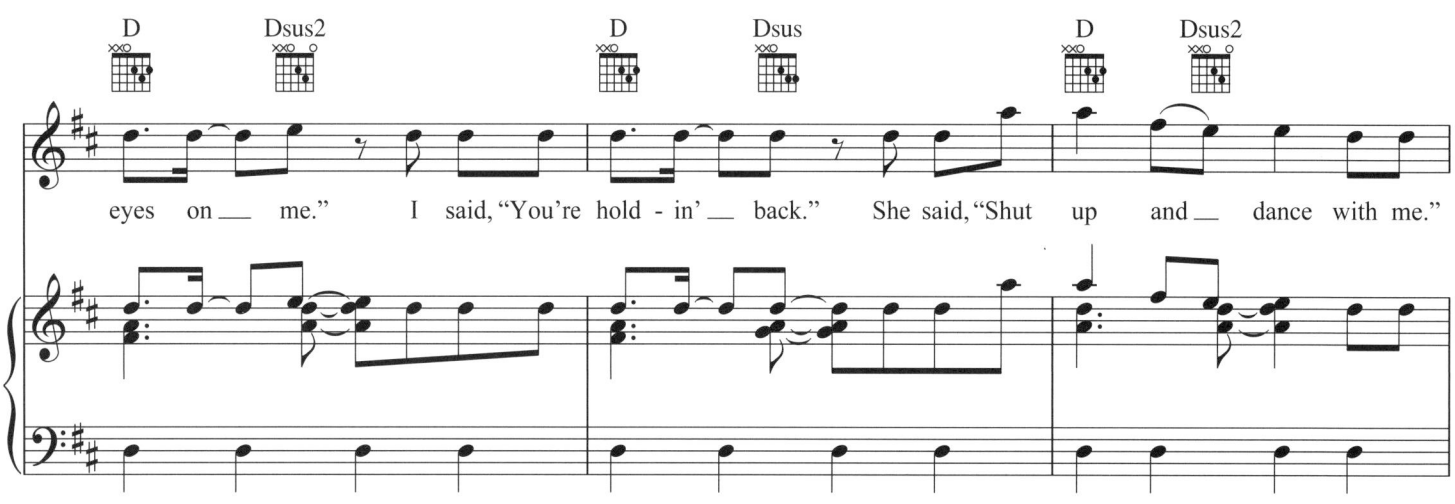

© 2014 WB MUSIC CORP., RYAN McMAHON PUBLISHING, BENJAMIN BERGER PUBLISHING, SONY/ATV MUSIC PUBLISHING LLC,
EMI APRIL MUSIC INC., ANNA SUN MUSIC, TREAT ME BETTER TINA MUSIC, VERB TO BE MUSIC and WHAT A RAUCOUS MUSIC
All Rights for RYAN McMAHON PUBLISHING and BENJAMIN BERGER PUBLISHING Administered by WB MUSIC CORP.
All Rights for SONY/ATV MUSIC PUBLISHING LLC, EMI APRIL MUSIC INC., ANNA SUN MUSIC, TREAT ME BETTER TINA MUSIC, VERB TO BE MUSIC
and WHAT A RAUCOUS MUSIC Administered by SONY/ATV MUSIC PUBLISHING LLC, 424 Church Street, Suite 1200, Nashville, TN 37219
All Rights Reserved   Used by Permission

A SKY FULL OF STARS

Words and Music by GUY BERRYMAN, JON BUCKLAND, WILL CHAMPION, CHRIS MARTIN and TIM BERGLING

Moderate Dance groove

'Cause you're a sky, _____ 'cause you're a
'Cause you're a sky, _____ 'cause you're a

sky _____ full of stars. _____
sky _____ full of stars. _____
                                        I'm gon-na
                                        I wan-na

give _____ you my heart. _____
die _____ in your arms. _____

Copyright © 2014 by Universal Music Publishing MGB Ltd. and EMI Blackwood Music Inc.
All Rights for Universal Music Publishing MGB Ltd. in the United States and Canada Administered by Universal Music - MGB Songs
All Rights for EMI Blackwood Music Inc. Administered by Sony/ATV Music Publishing LLC, 424 Church Street, Suite 1200, Nashville, TN 37219
International Copyright Secured   All Rights Reserved

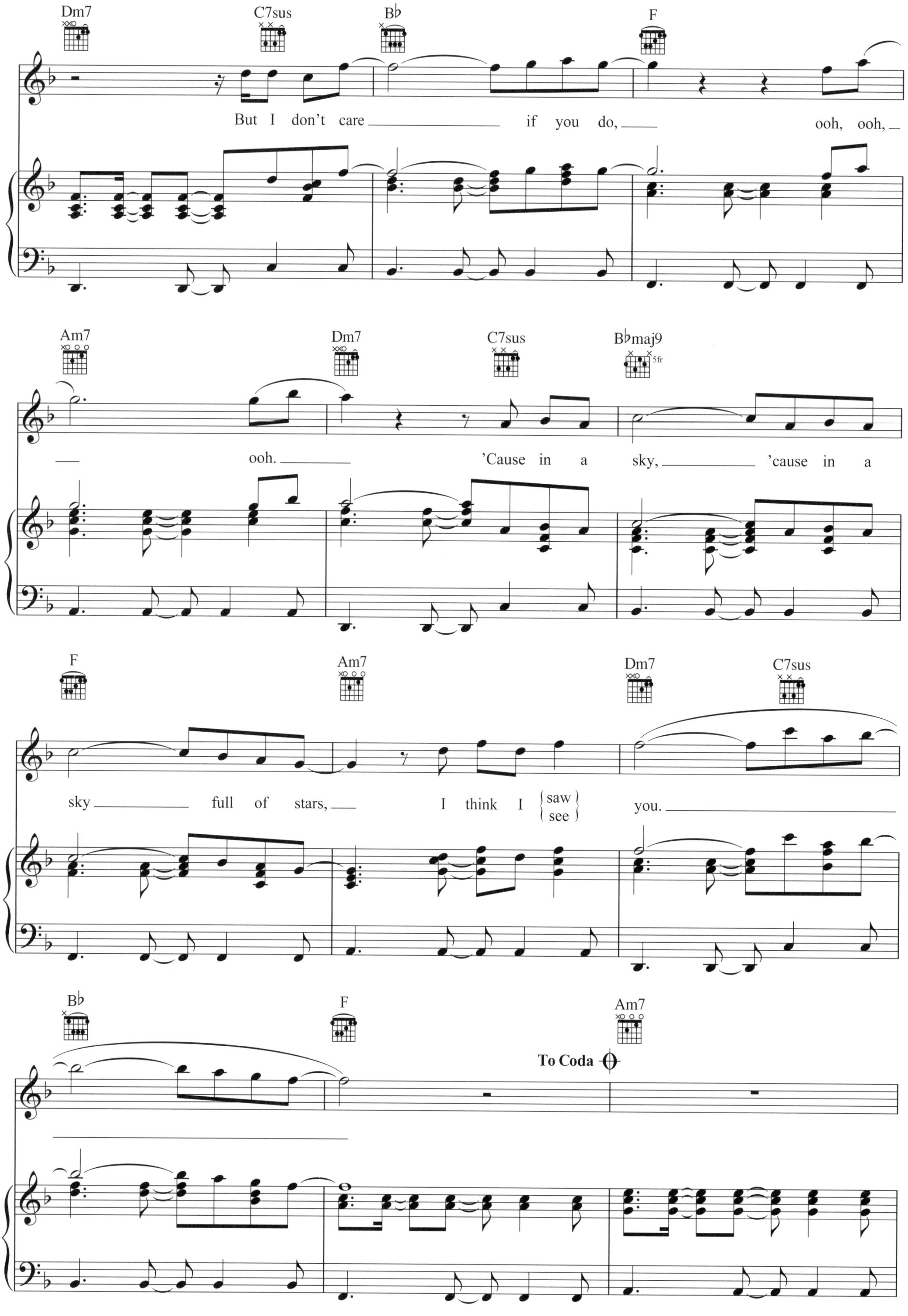
Dm7
C7sus
B♭
F
But I don't care if you do, ooh, ooh,
Am7
Dm7
C7sus
B♭maj9
5fr
ooh. 'Cause in a sky, 'cause in a
F
Am7
Dm7
C7sus
sky full of stars, I think I {saw / see} you.
B♭
F
Am7
To Coda

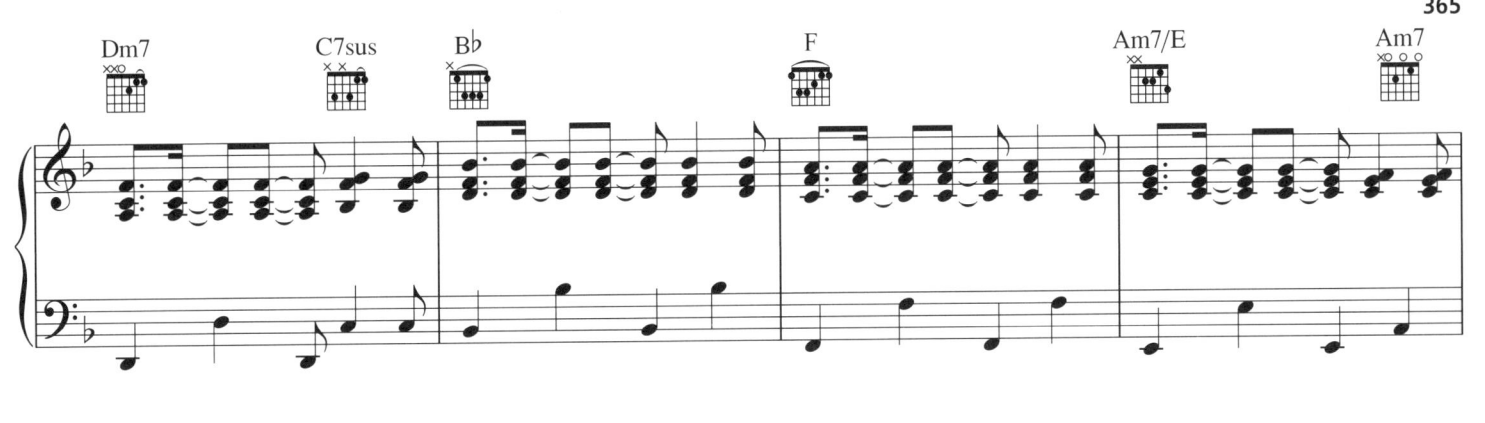

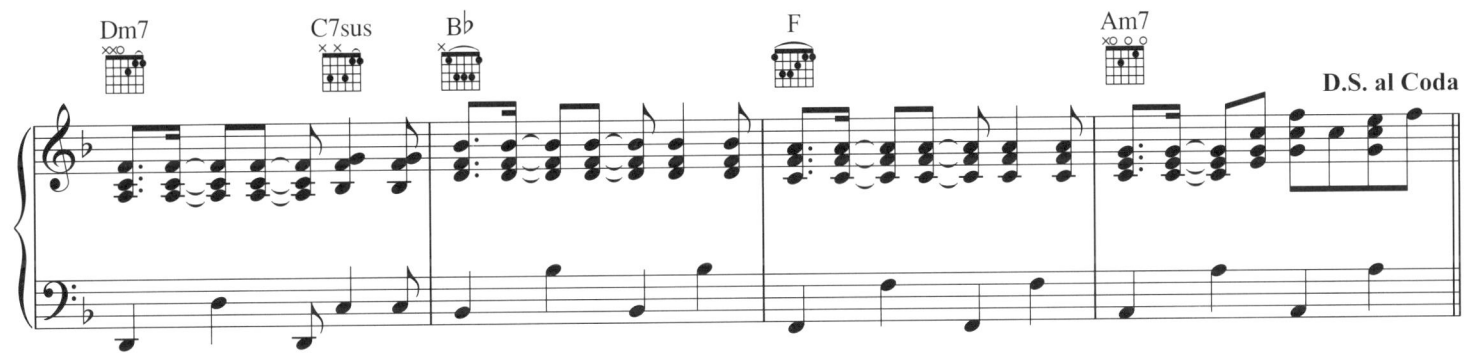
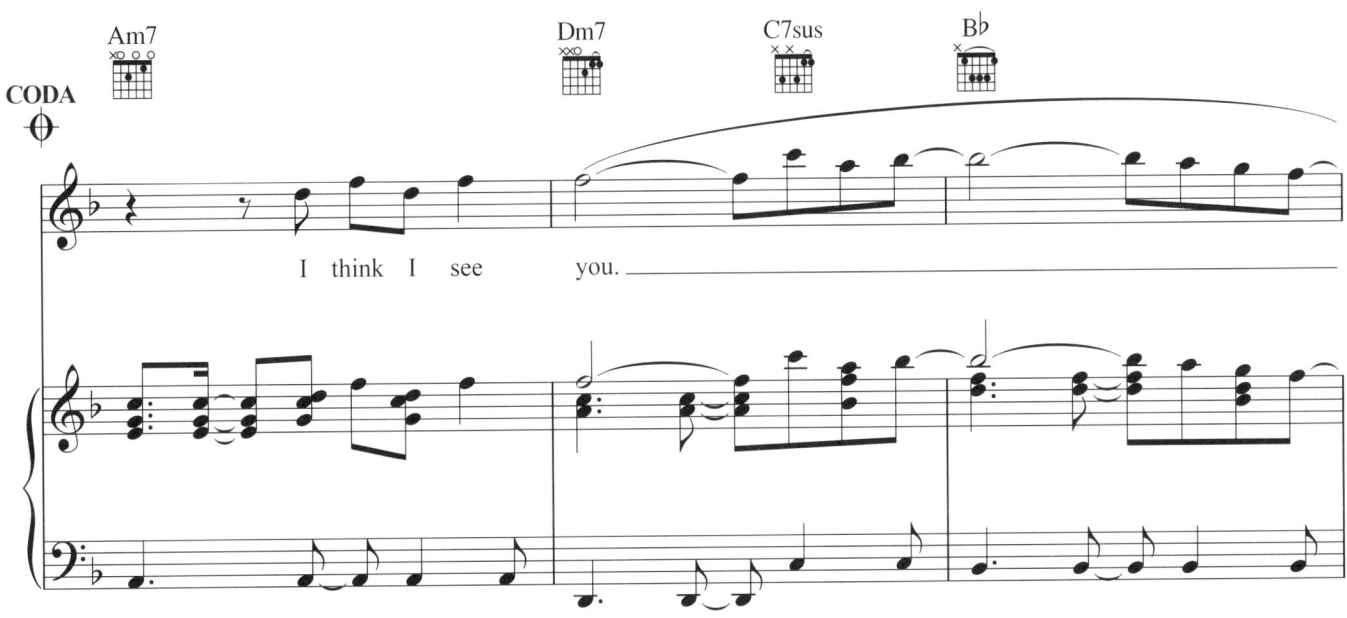

I think I see you.

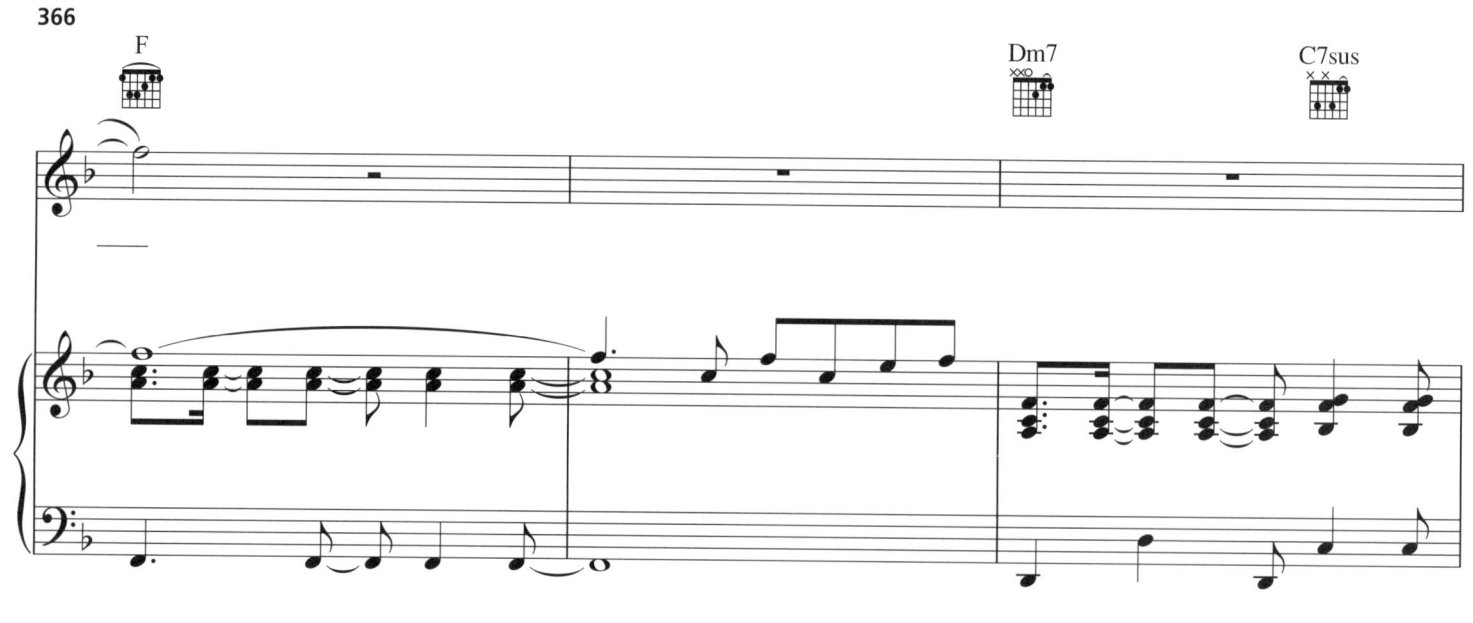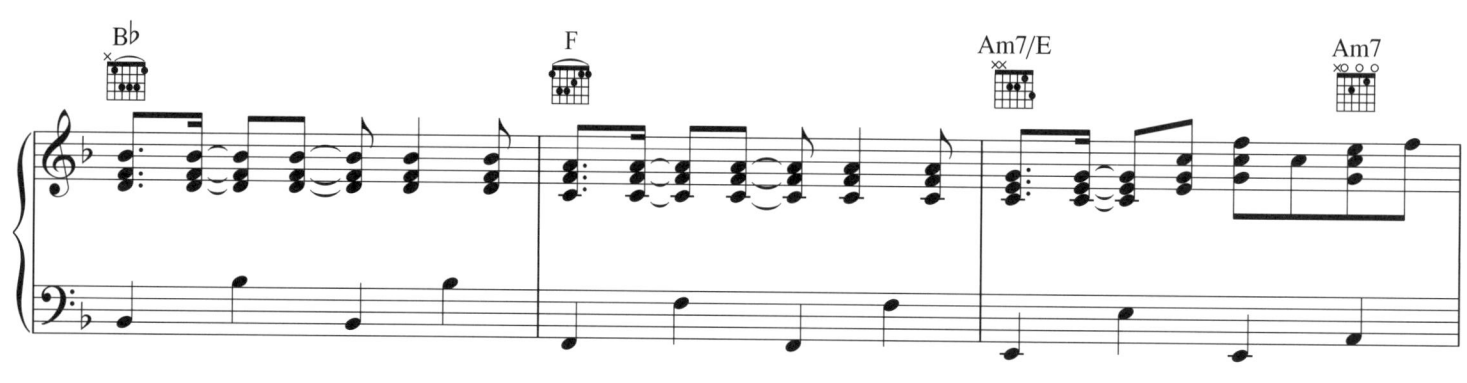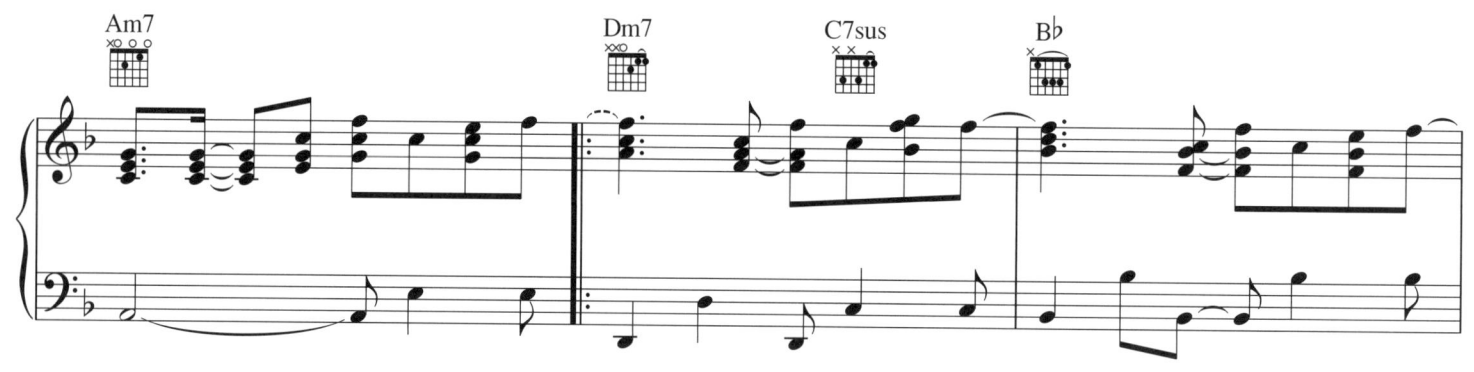

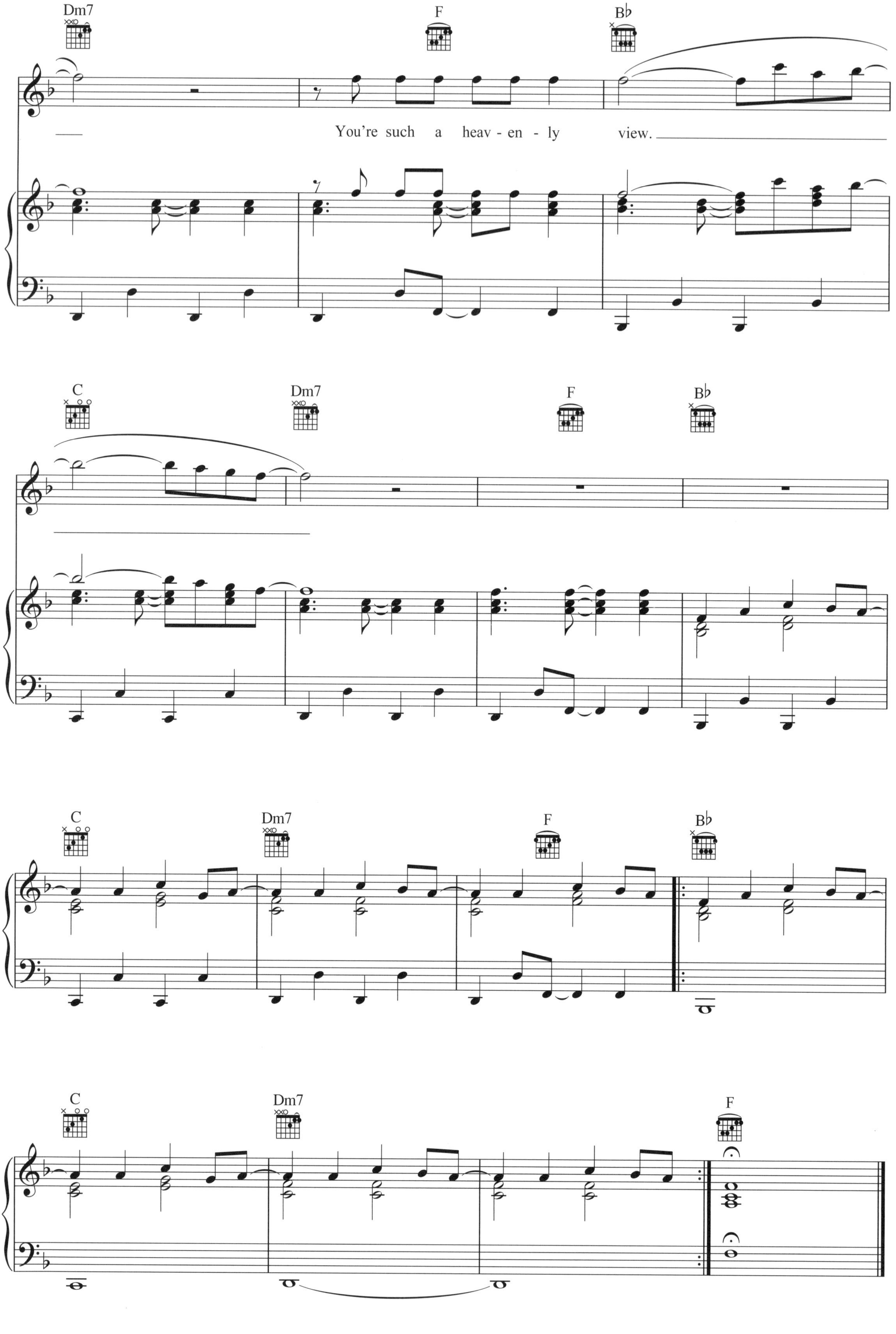
Dm7
F
B♭
You're such a heav - en - ly view.
C
Dm7
F
B♭
C
Dm7
F
B♭
C
Dm7
F

STRONGER
(What Doesn't Kill You)

Words and Music by GREG KURSTIN,
JORGEN ELOFSSON, DAVID GAMSON
and ALEXANDRA TAMPOSI

© 2011 EMI APRIL MUSIC INC., KURSTIN MUSIC, UNIVERSAL MUSIC PUBLISHING MGB SCANDINAVIA, BMG GOLD SONGS and PERFECT STORM MUSIC GROUP AB
All Rights for KURSTIN MUSIC Controlled and Administered by EMI APRIL MUSIC INC.
All Rights for UNIVERSAL MUSIC PUBLISHING MGB SCANDINAVIA in the United States and Canada Administered by UNIVERSAL MUSIC - CAREERS
All Rights for BMG GOLD SONGS Administered by BMG RIGHTS MANAGEMENT (US) LLC
All Rights for PERFECT STORM MUSIC GROUP AB Administered by SONY/ATV MUSIC PUBLISHING LLC, 424 Church Street, Suite 1200, Nashville, TN 37219
All Rights Reserved   International Copyright Secured   Used by Permission

SOME NIGHTS

Words and Music by JEFF BHASKER, ANDREW DOST, JACK ANTONOFF and NATE RUESS

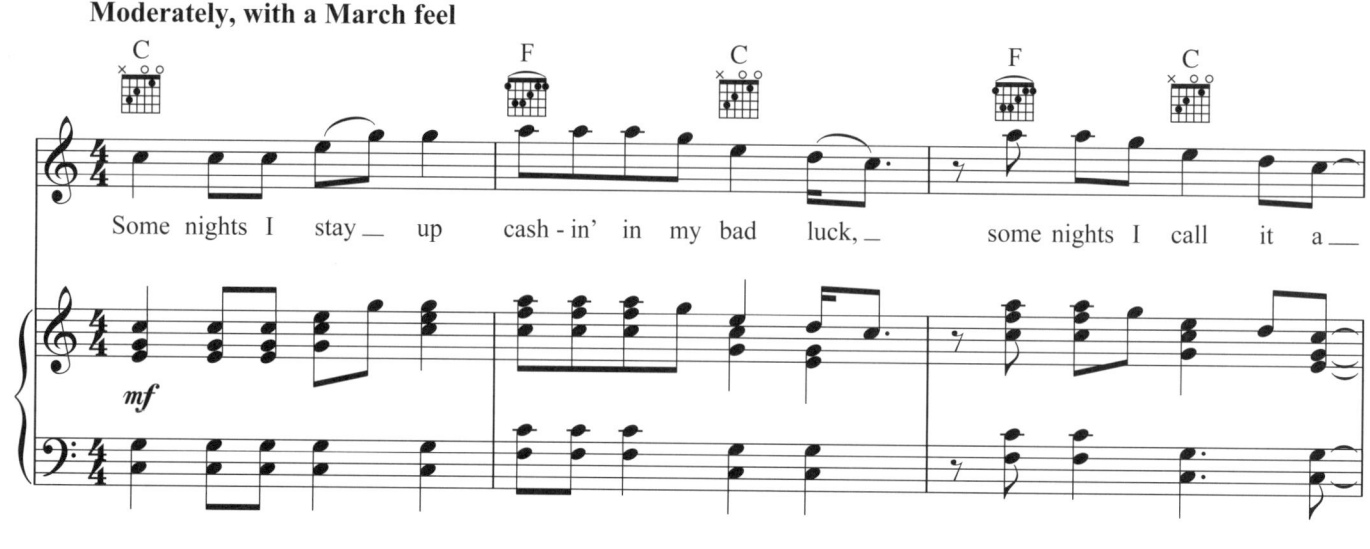

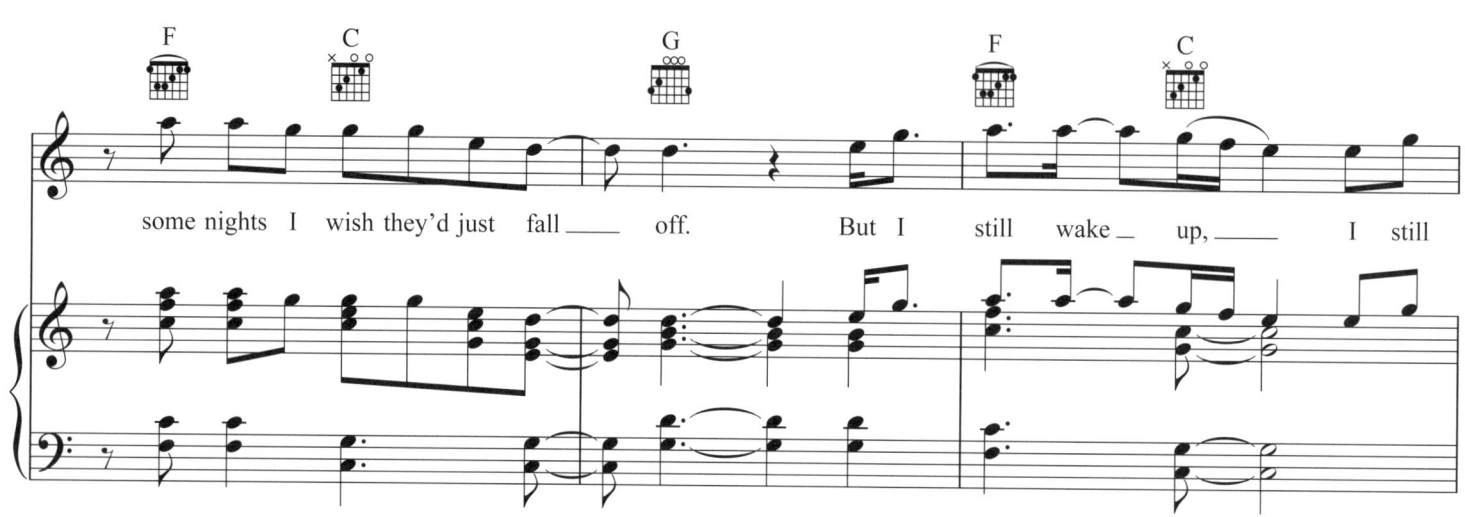

Copyright © 2012 Sony/ATV Music Publishing LLC, Way Above Music, Rough Art, Shira Lee Lawrence Rick Music, WB Music Corp., FBR Music and Bearvon Music
All Rights on behalf of Sony/ATV Music Publishing LLC, Way Above Music, Rough Art and Shira Lee Lawrence Rick Music Administered by
Sony/ATV Music Publishing LLC, 424 Church Street, Suite 1200, Nashville, TN 37219
All Rights on behalf of FBR Music and Bearvon Music Administered by WB Music Corp.
International Copyright Secured   All Rights Reserved

SOMEONE LIKE YOU

Words and Music by ADELE ADKINS
and DAN WILSON

STAY

Words and Music by MIKKY EKKO and JUSTIN PARKER

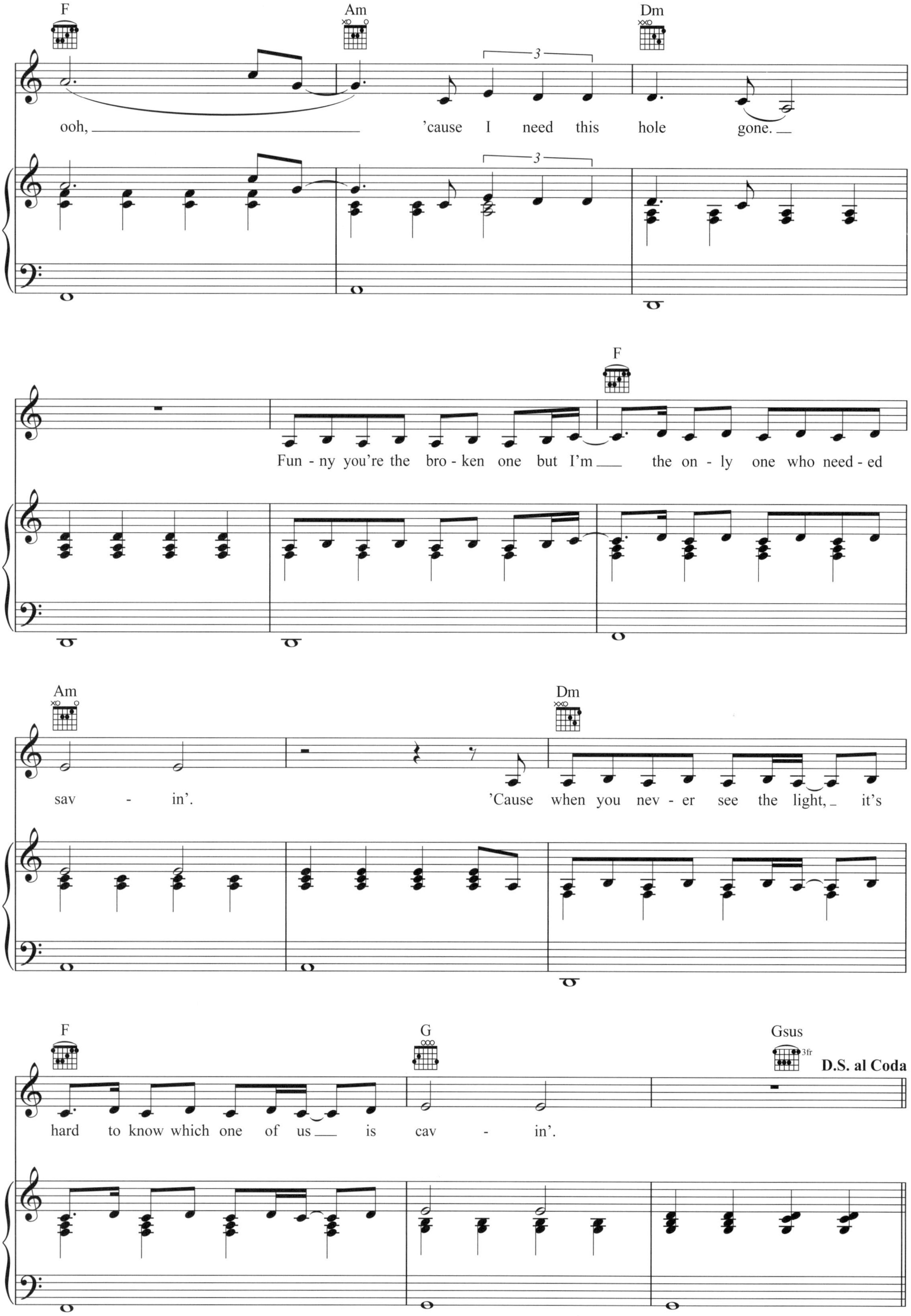
F
Am
Dm
ooh, 'cause I need this hole gone.
F
Fun - ny you're the bro - ken one but I'm the on - ly one who need - ed
Am
Dm
sav - in'. 'Cause when you nev - er see the light, it's
F
G
Gsus
D.S. al Coda
hard to know which one of us is cav - in'.

TAKE ME TO CHURCH

Words and Music by
ANDREW HOZIER-BYRNE

My lover's got humour, she's the giggle at a fun'ral.

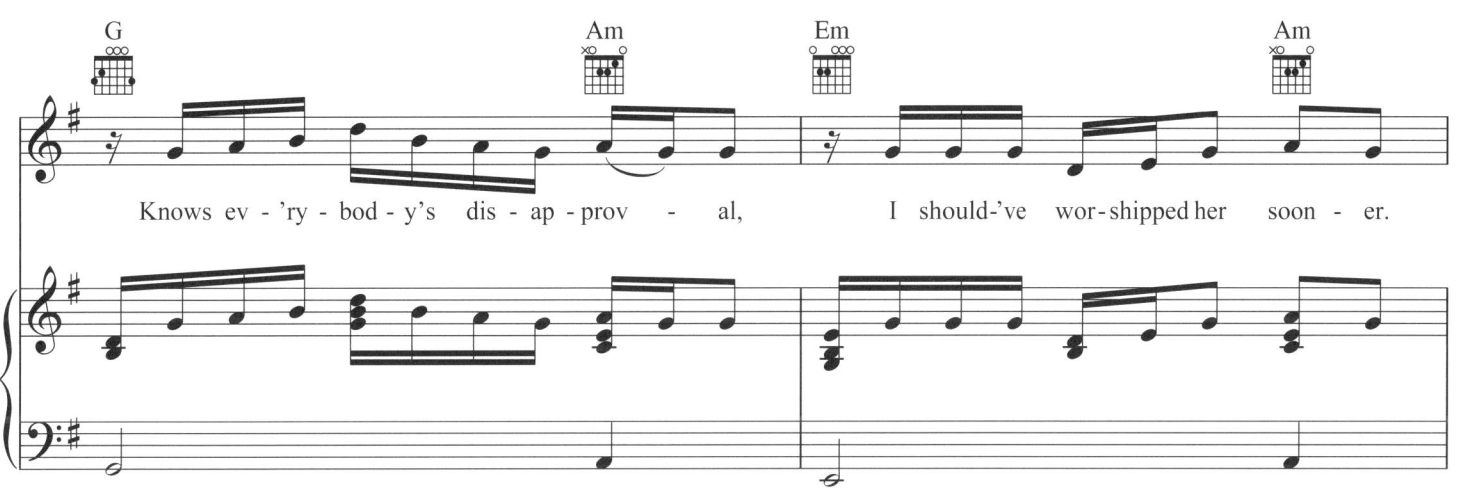

Knows ev'rybody's disapproval, I should've worshipped her sooner.

If the heavens ever did speak, she's the last true mouthpiece. Ev'ry Sunday's getting more bleak,

Copyright © 2014 Sony/ATV Music Publishing LLC and The Evolving Music Company Limited
All Rights Administered by Sony/ATV Music Publishing LLC, 424 Church Street, Suite 1200, Nashville, TN 37219
International Copyright Secured All Rights Reserved

THINKING OUT LOUD

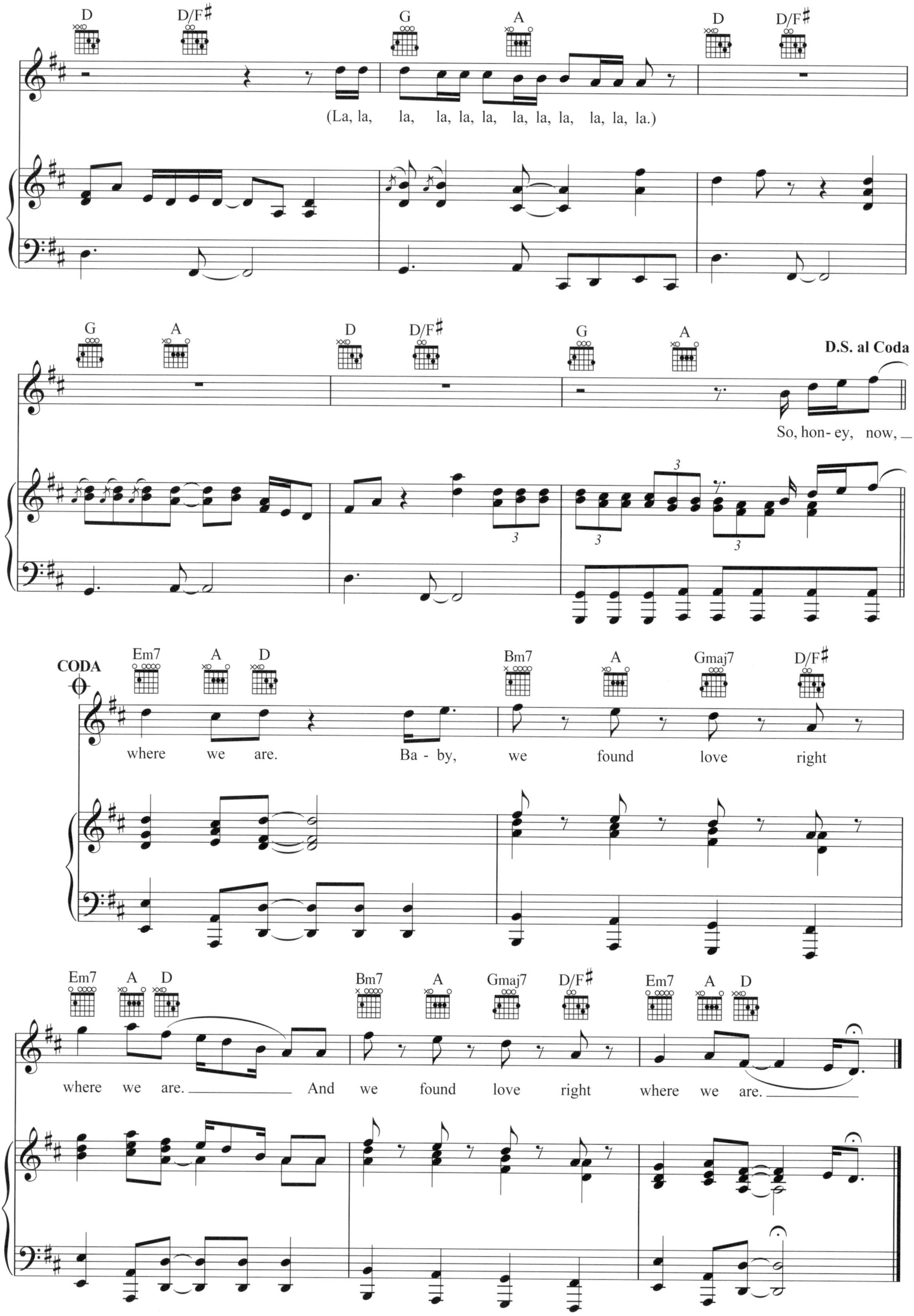
D D/F# G A D D/F#
(La, la, la, la, la, la, la, la, la, la, la, la.)
G A D D/F# G A
D.S. al Coda
So, hon- ey, now,
CODA
Em7 A D Bm7 A Gmaj7 D/F#
where we are. Ba - by, we found love right
Em7 A D Bm7 A Gmaj7 D/F# Em7 A D
where we are. And we found love right where we are.

A Thousand Years

from the Summit Entertainment film THE TWILIGHT SAGA: BREAKING DAWN – PART 1

Words and Music by DAVID HODGES
and CHRISTINA PERRI

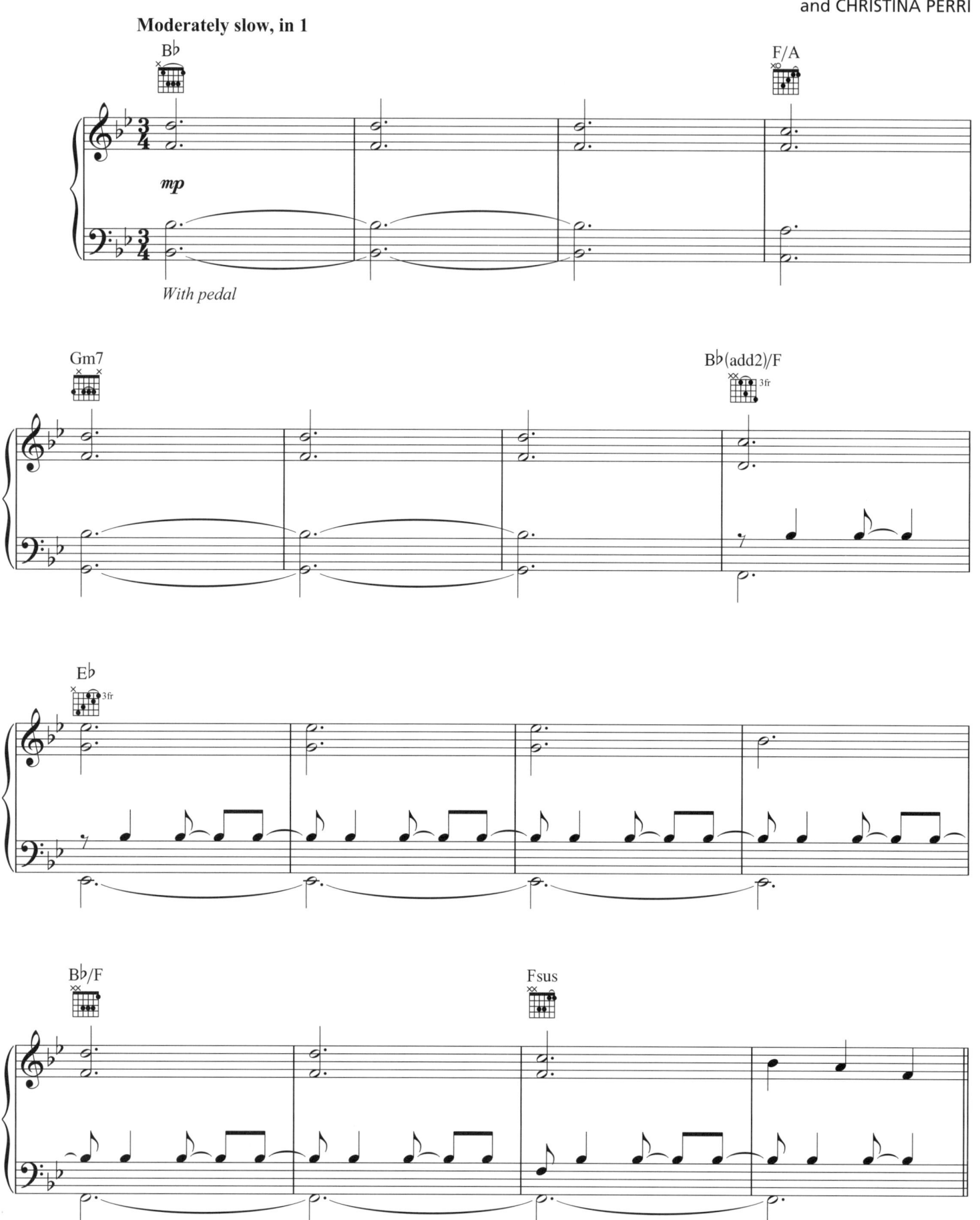

© 2011 EMI BLACKWOOD MUSIC INC., 12:06 PUBLISHING, MISS PERRI LANE PUBLISHING and SUMMIT BASE CAMP FILM MUSIC
All Rights for 12:06 PUBLISHING Controlled and Administered by EMI BLACKWOOD MUSIC INC.
All Rights for MISS PERRI LANE PUBLISHING Controlled and Administered by SONGS OF KOBALT MUSIC PUBLISHING
All Rights Reserved   International Copyright Secured   Used by Permission

TOO CLOSE

Words and Music by ALEX CLAIRE
and JIM DUGUID

Moderately fast

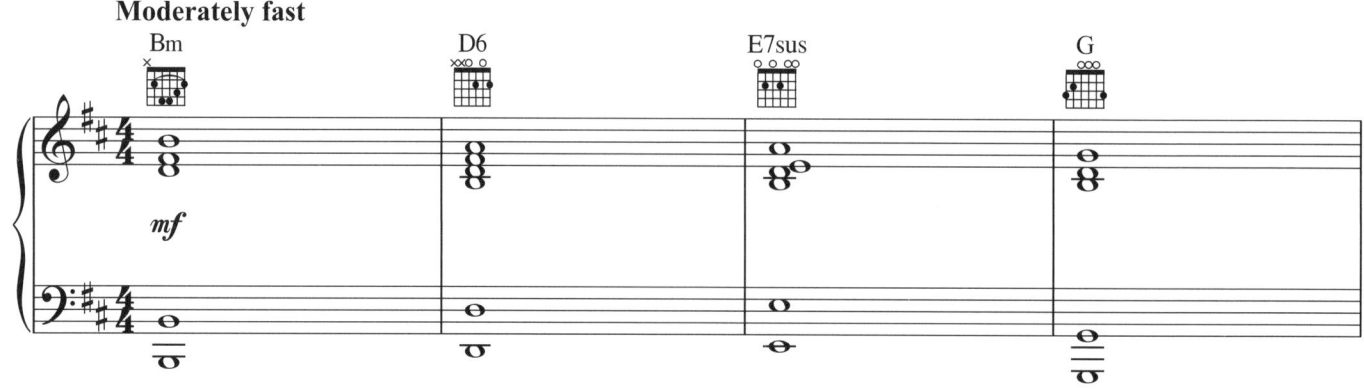
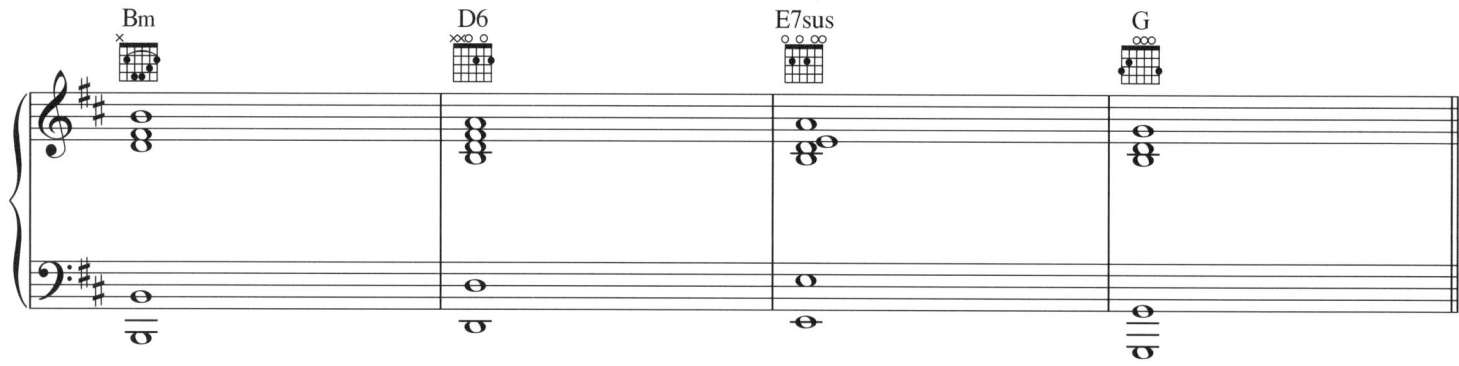
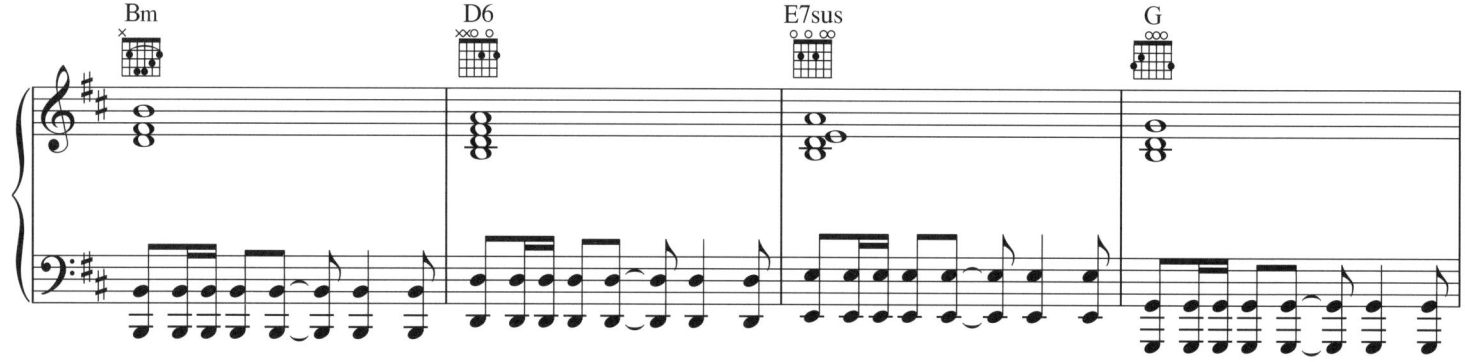
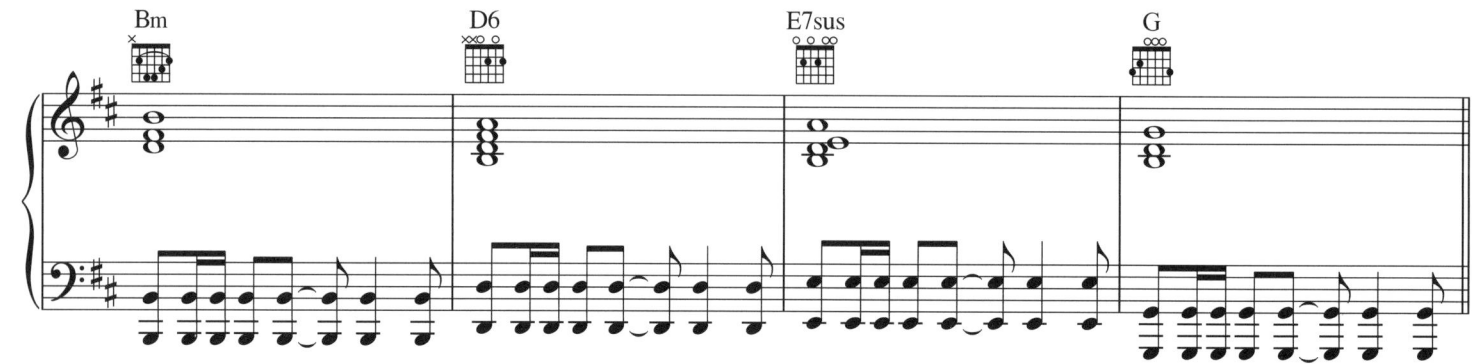

Copyright © 2010, 2011 UNIVERSAL MUSIC PUBLISHING PGM LTD. and WARNER-CHAPPELL MUSIC PUBLISHING LTD.
All Rights for UNIVERSAL MUSIC PUBLISHING PGM LTD. in the U.S. and Canada Controlled and Administered by UNIVERSAL - POLYGRAM INTERNATIONAL PUBLISHING, INC.
All Rights for WARNER/CHAPPELL MUSIC PUBLISHING LTD. in the U.S. and Canada Administered by WB MUSIC CORP.
All Rights Reserved   Used by Permission

WAKE ME UP!

Words and Music by ALOE BLACC,
TIM BERGLING and MICHAEL EINZIGER

© 2013 WB MUSIC CORP., ALOE BLACC PUBLISHING, EMI MUSIC PUBLISHING SCANDINAVIA AB, UNIVERSAL MUSIC CORP. and ELEMENTARY PARTICLE MUSIC
All Rights on behalf of itself and ALOE BLACC PUBLISHIING Administered by WB MUSIC CORP.
All Rights on behalf of EMI MUSIC PUBLISHING SCANDINAVIA AB Administered by SONY/ATV MUSIC PUBLISHING LLC, 424 Church Street, Suite 1200, Nashville, TN 37219
All Rights on behalf of ELEMENTARY PARTICLE MUSIC Controlled and Administered by UNIVERSAL MUSIC CORP.
All Rights Reserved   Used by Permission

WE ARE YOUNG

Words and Music by JEFF BHASKER,
ANDREW DOST, JACK ANTONOFF
and NATE RUESS

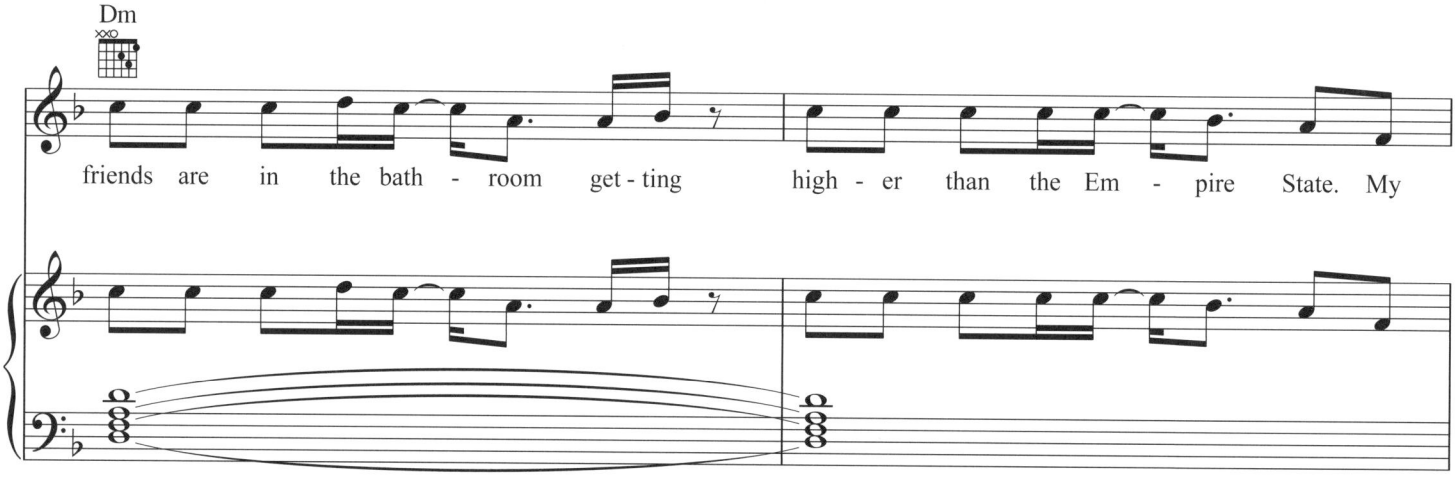

Copyright © 2011, 2012 Sony/ATV Music Publishing LLC, Way Above Music, Rough Art, Shira Lee Lawrence Rick Music, WB Music Corp., FBR Music and Bearvon Music
All Rights on behalf of Sony/ATV Music Publishing LLC, Way Above Music, Rough Art and Shira Lee Lawrence Rick Music Administered by
Sony/ATV Music Publishing LLC, 424 Church Street, Suite 1200, Nashville, TN 37219
All Rights on behalf of FBR Music and Bearvon Music Administered by WB Music Corp.
International Copyright Secured   All Rights Reserved

WHAT MAKES YOU BEAUTIFUL

Words and Music by SAVAN KOTECHA,
RAMI YACOUB and CARL FALK

Moderate Pop

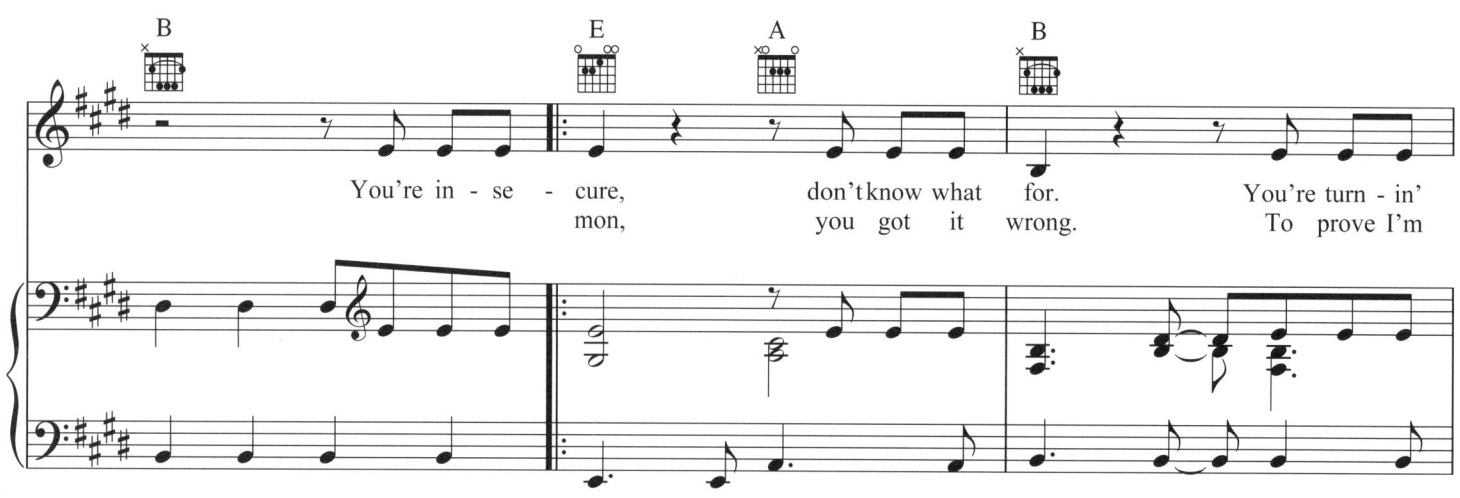

You're in - se - cure, don't know what for.   You're turn - in'
mon,   you got it wrong.   To prove I'm

heads when you walk through the do - o - or.   Don't need make - up   to cov - er
right, I put it in a so - o - ong.   I don't know why   you're be - ing

© 2011 EMI APRIL MUSIC INC., KOBALT MUSIC COPYRIGHTS SARL and BMG RIGHTS MANAGEMENT SCANDINAVIA AB
All Rights for BMG RIGHTS MANAGEMENT SCANDINAVIA AB Administered by BMG RIGHTS MANAGEMENT (US) LLC
All Rights Reserved   International Copyright Secured   Used by Permission

light up my world like nobody else. The way that you flip your hair gets me
overwhelmed. But when you smile at the ground it ain't
hard to tell you don't know oh-oh, you don't know you're beautiful.
Baby, you

light up my world like nobody else. The way that
If only you saw what I can see, you'll under-

UPTOWN FUNK

Words and Music by MARK RONSON,
BRUNO MARS, PHILIP LAWRENCE,
JEFF BHASKER, DEVON GALLASPY,
NICHOLAUS WILLIAMS, LONNIE SIMMONS,
RONNIE WILSON, CHARLES WILSON,
RUDOLPH TAYLOR and ROBERT WILSON

Copyright © 2014 by Songs Of Zelig, Imagem CV, BMG Gold Songs, Mars Force Music, WB Music Corp., Thou Art The Hunger, ZZR Music LLC,
Sony/ATV Songs LLC, Way Above Music, Sony/ATV Ballad, TIG7 Publishing, Trinlanta Publishing and Taking Care Of Business Music, Inc.
All Rights for Songs Of Zelig and Imagem CV Administered by Songs Of Imagem Music
All Rights for BMG Gold Songs and Mars Force Music Administered by BMG Rights Management (US) LLC
All Rights for Thou Art The Hunger Administered by WB Music Corp.
All Rights for ZZR Music LLC Administered by Universal Music Corp.
All Rights for Sony/ATV Songs LLC, Way Above Music and Sony/ATV Ballad Administered by Sony/ATV Music Publishing LLC, 424 Church Street, Suite 1200, Nashville, TN 37219
All Rights Reserved   Used by Permission
- interpolates "All Gold Everything" performed by Trinidad James © 2015 Songs Music Publishing, LLC o/b/o Trinlanta Publishing, TIG7 Publishing and Songs MP, used with permission

475

480